Counselling and Psychotherapy
with Refugees

of related interest

Arts Therapists, Refugees and Migrants
Reaching Across Borders
Edited by Ditty Dokter
Foreword by Dick Blackwell
ISBN 1 85302 550 X

A House Next Door to Trauma
Learning from Holocaust Survivors How to Respond to
Atrocity
Judith Hassan
ISBN 1 85302 867 3

Trauma, the Body and Transformation
A Narrative Inquiry
Edited by Kim Etherington
ISBN 1 84310 106 8

Psychodrama with Trauma Survivors
Acting Out Your Pain
Edited by Peter Felix Kellermann and M. K. Hudgins
Foreword by Zerka T. Moreno
ISBN 1 85302 893 2

Social Work, Immigration and Asylum
Debates, Dilemmas and Ethical Issues for Social Work and
Social Care Practice
Edited by Debra Hayes and Beth Humphries
Foreword by Steve Cohen
ISBN 1 84310 194 7

Immigration Controls, the Family and the Welfare State
A Handbook of Law, Theory, Politics and Practice for
Local Authority, Voluntary Sector and Welfare State
Workers and Legal Advisors
Steve Cohen
ISBN 1 85302 723 5

Counselling and Psychotherapy with Refugees

Dick Blackwell

Jessica Kingsley Publishers
London and Philadelphia

The right of Dick Blackwell to be identified as author of this work has been asserted by him in accordance with the Copyright, Designs and Patents Act 1988.

First published in 2005
by Jessica Kingsley Publishers
116 Pentonville Road
London N1 9JB, UK
and
400 Market Street, Suite 400
Philadelphia, PA 19106, USA

www.jkp.com

Copyright © Dick Blackwell 2005

Library of Congress Cataloging in Publication Data
A CIP catalog record for this book is available from the Library of Congress

British Library Cataloguing in Publication Data
A CIP catalogue record for this book is available from the British Library

ISBN-13: 978 1 84310 316 5
ISBN-10: 1 84310 316 8

Printed and Bound in Great Britain by
Athenaeum Press, Gateshead, Tyne and Wear

Contents

Acknowledgements

This is not a field in which one gets very far alone, nor indeed one in which going it alone is very advisable. The stresses are too great, the issues are too big and the field of knowledge too broad. This book has therefore been shaped by the contributions of many colleagues over many years.

When I first began working at the Medical Foundation for the Care of Victims of Torture and Organised Violence over 15 years ago, there were few staff, even fewer psychotherapists and no supervision. It was a case of pitching in and learning by the seat of one's pants.

I knew something about how to do psychotherapy in general, I knew something about global politics and political history, and I knew something about culture and the problems of cross-cultural psychotherapy. But I knew next to nothing about refugees nor about the personal and interpersonal impact of the traumatic events most of them experienced in the course of becoming refugees. So after I had seen my clients I would prowl the corridors of the Medical Foundation (MF) in search of some insight, advice, suggestions, ideas or anything else that might give me some idea whether I was anywhere near being on the right track. Sometimes I found the director Helen Bamber's door open. More often I would wander into Perico Rodriguez's office. Perico was a political activist and subsequently a political prisoner in Argentina who had joined the Foundation some time before me. He would listen patiently to my efforts at making sense of my clients' experiences and would generously draw on his own personal and professional experience to try to reduce my level of ignorance. He also shared with me his political analysis and helped me connect my own political perceptions with the psychotherapeutic work. Some time later when he and another colleague set up a counselling/psychotherapy group for Latin Americans he asked me, as a group analyst, to provide supervision for them. What I don't think he realized was that it was him who up to that point had been supervising me.

A year or so later we were joined at the Foundation by another refugee, Erol Yesilyurt from Turkey. He had a similar capacity to Perico's to link the personal, the interpersonal, the cultural and the political, and was similarly generous in his readiness to contribute his personal experiences to my attempts to grasp the connections between these domains.

Much of this book is based on the understanding and the conceptual framework I began developing in those early meetings and discussions with Perico and Erol.

I first worked with Sheila Melzak in 1990 when we were co-coordinators of the first group of volunteer psychotherapists. Subsequently we worked together on a clinical research project sponsored jointly by the Medical Foundation and the Child Psychotherapy Trust. This book owes much to the ideas we have developed in this work with children and families.

Rachel Tribe recruited me as a co-conductor of supervision groups she was setting up for volunteer caseworker/counsellors at the Foundation. As this work developed the emphasis shifted from a predominant focus on casework and advocacy, addressed to the clients' current material needs, to a focus on the needs of the clients to talk about their experiences and try to make some sort of sense of what had happened to them. So they became counsellor/caseworkers, and I am grateful to Rachel and to all the members of those groups over the last 14 years for bringing me into contact with such a wide range of therapeutic work, and contributing their own ideas and insights to the picture I have been developing. When Rachel left the Foundation, Gill Hinshelwood replaced her as co-conductor of these supervision groups and helped me think in greater depth about the intrapsychic experiences of both clients and therapists.

Other valuable contributions to my thinking have come from Marika Lindbom Jacobson from Stockholm, who worked with me on countertransference; Zoran Bozovic, who consulted with me on his work with Bosnian refugees; and Derek Summerfield, who provided a challenging critique of western approaches to non-western cultures.

Too numerous to mention by name are all the counsellors and psychotherapists who have volunteered their services over the last 15 years and whom I have had the privilege of coordinating and supervising. It is the discussion and analysis of their work and our struggles together in those supervision groups that have provided the range of clients' experiences, clinicians' experiences and the variety of approaches that have informed the book.

Conversation between clients and therapists who do not speak the same language would not be possible without interpreters. Those members of the Medical Foundation's team of interpreters who have participated in my own therapeutic work have been invaluable in not only translating the spoken words but also in explaining cultural differences and historical contexts.

Over the last seven years there has been a fortnightly meeting of supervisors of counselling and psychotherapy in the Foundation. This has been an extraordinary group whose discussions have ranged from the psychodynamics and administrative practicalities of supervision (individual and group), across global political developments and their impact on our clients, our supervisees and ourselves, to the political context of the UK in which we work, and the institutional countertransferences which affect the internal structures and processes of our organization. The convenor John Schlapobersky, and the members Jeremy Woodcock, Sheila Melzak, Gill Hinshelwood, Helen Bamber, Rami Heilbron, Phyllis Goldblatt, Jocelyn Avigad and Karen Callaghan, have provided a remarkable range of experience and expertise, and a quality of thought and dialogue that has contributed much to the development of the approach described here. Additionally they all read and discussed my original draft.

I received further commentaries on that draft from David Kennard from the Retreat in York; Jude Boyles, who was in the process of recruiting counsellors and psychotherapists to work with torture survivors in the north of England; Emma Williams, MF

Regional Development Officer; Janet Myers, of the Brighton and Hove Refugee Project; and Judy Hildebrand, formerly of the Institute of Family Therapy and the Tavistock Clinic, who not only provided comments as a family therapist and trainer but also did a thorough job of editing the whole text.

I am grateful to all of the above for their various contributions, for their ideas, for their support and encouragement, for their criticism and disagreement, for their sometimes extraordinary energy and commitment, all of which has informed and enriched my work. I am also grateful to Anju Mittu at the Medical Foundation who deciphered my handwriting to type the first draft.

Most importantly we are all indebted to the clients of the Medical Foundation who have allowed us to participate in their struggles and helped us to learn how.

Part I

Setting the Scene: Openings and Engagements

CHAPTER 1

Who and What This Book is For

This book is for anyone doing counselling or psychotherapy with refugees. It is based on work undertaken at the Medical Foundation for the Care of Victims of Torture and Organised Violence and represents an attempt to generalize some of what we have learned through this work and share it with colleagues in other settings.

It was originally prompted by the UK government's policy of dispersing refugees to different parts of the UK rather than allowing them to stay in London. This dispersal has had two consequences.

First, it moves many refugees away from refugee communities which have developed in the capital, London, so there is less support available from extended family and fellow nationals who share the problem of exile and adjustment to a new society and culture. This increases the likelihood that they will need professional help.

Second, it moves many refugees away from specialist refugee agencies; so if they need counselling and psycho-therapy they must seek it in areas where there is often relatively little in the way of existing expertise. Many requests have been made from around the UK to my organization (the Medical Foundation for the Care of Victims of Torture) for advice, information, consultation and training. It was in response to that need that this book was first conceived.

However, once the book took shape, it became clear that it could be of use to a wider readership, including fellow counsellors and psychotherapists already working in the field.

It was intended to be a brief introductory text to provide professionals in the field with a basic framework within which to think and work, and to help them get a feel for where their clients are coming from. It is not a 'how to do it' book. It is more an attempt to outline the sort of experiences clients have, and the sort of experiences counsellors and psychotherapists have in response, so that the therapist may be better able to make sense of what is going on both for him or herself and for his or her clients. I believe that as counsellors and psychotherapists, we all have to work in our own way, so I have tried to offer a framework which facilitates therapists finding their own way of engaging with their clients.

I use the term 'therapist' generally to cover both counsellor and psychotherapist and I have not attempted to distinguish between counselling and psychotherapy. While I appreciate that many practitioners regard this distinction as important, my emphasis here is not on describing a particular model of working but on providing a context which I think is generally relevant whatever therapeutic model is practised. Moreover, my aim here is to facilitate adaptation: that is, the adaptation and tailoring of specific models of therapy to meet the requirements of working with this specific client group. In some parts of what follows, aspects of my own psychodynamic orientation will be quite evident. I hope that those who do not share, or even dispute, some of these ideas will not be put off by this but will share my commitment to make the model, whatever it is, relevant to the experiences of the clients.

The book begins (Part I) with a brief outline of how I see the place of counselling and psychotherapy in relation to refugees: that is, briefly summarized, they may not all need it, but a significant number might want it; and it is one of their human rights to have it made available to them if they do want it. Additionally, refugees do not have any specific or characteristic psychopathology but they do have certain typical experiences of persecution, violence and flight into exile and it helps if counsellors and psychotherapists understand something about those experiences.

The main section (Parts II and III) of the book is divided into two parts. The first deals with the refugees' experiences and the second deals with the therapists' experiences. (Both parts include the way that refugees experience counsellors and the way that counsellors experience refugees.)

In each part, I have addressed four dimensions or levels of experience: the political, the cultural, the interpersonal and the intrapsychic. Initially I thought it was technically more precise to use the term 'dimensions' of experience rather than 'levels', which seemed to convey some sort of hierarchy. However, I have on reflection decided to call them 'levels of experience' because that is how I think of them. I also realized that I *do* think of them in terms of a hierarchy. Politics is the way society is organized and it provides the framework for culture to develop. It is that culture which in turn provides the language and symbols of interpersonal communication. Individual personality and interiority develop in the context of interpersonal communication, culture and politics.

The relationship between the levels is not deterministic and one way. It is reciprocally influential. Cultural change can influence politics; and individuals can influence politics and culture. Nor do I intend to imply four discrete areas of experience. I am separating them out for the purpose of exposition and understanding. But, obviously, a single conscious thought or unconscious phantasy may be political, cultural and interpersonal. One has only to think of the immorality laws during 'Apartheid' in South Africa to recognize that. Similarly, at the time of writing, the Israel/Palestine situation gives any interpersonal contact between any Jew and any Palestinian an obvious political significance. My framework is therefore a way of looking at different levels of social and psychological discourse, different levels of human life and recognizing the way they are part of the matrix of experience through which we all become, and go on becoming, who we are.

In Part IV, there are three additional chapters (plus a summary). One is on working with interpreters, which will be a new experience for many counsellors and psychotherapists. The next, on 'advocacy', addresses the work a therapist may be called on to do in relation to the client's asylum application, welfare rights and other material needs, which are outside the normal remit of counsellors and psychotherapists but which may, in work with refugees, become necessary in order to preserve the context in which counselling or psychotherapy can take place: that is, to enable the client to be in a position to come for therapy and make some use of it.

The penultimate chapter on supervision was interestingly not part of the original draft but added some 18 months later when it finally occurred to me that I had missed one of the most important aspects of this work, and one of the most frequently overlooked. This chapter looks at the need for supervision, some characteristic dynamics of the supervisory process in work with refugees, and the different supervisory structures which might be applied.

The last thing I want to say, by way of introduction, is that I do not want to paint a picture of refugees as some sort of alien persons who are so different from us that we need books by 'experts' to help us understand them. They are people who have gone through particular experiences to which they will have responded in a variety of ways. As counsellors and psychotherapists, our work, or at least a large part of it, is the struggle to find words to articulate and give meaning to human experience. But the words can never fully capture the whole experience. Similarly the 'otherness' of the 'other' constantly escapes our grasp even as we discover how like ourselves the other actually is. It is our similarities that enable us to communicate, and it is our 'otherness' that makes our communication necessary. And, of course, if we take seriously our professed belief in the unconscious (those of us who *do* believe in it), we are always, in some important sense, 'other' to ourselves. Thus, whenever we talk about 'us' and 'them', 'we' are always more 'other' to each other than we like to imagine, and 'they' are always another collection of others, not only more 'other' to each other but also more like ourselves than we are prepared to concede.

CHAPTER 2

Counselling, Psychotherapy and the Refugee Experience

The purpose of this book is emphatically not to propose that refugees suffer some particular form of pathology for which they are going to need counselling and psychotherapy – nor, indeed, is it to suggest that all refugees will need some sort of counselling.

I do not believe in counselling and psychotherapy in this or any other context as treatment for some sort of illness or pathology. Counselling and psychotherapy are aids in the struggles of living: struggles in which all of us are engaged by virtue of being alive. Many people manage their lives quite happily and successfully without counselling or psychotherapy. Others feel the need for it and choose to avail themselves of it. Having counselling or psychotherapy is a subjective existential choice. It is not necessarily predicated on any so-called objective assessment of need for psychotherapy, but on the lived experience of the subject, who decides to avail him or herself of it. Refugees in general are people for whom life has got particularly tough. For this reason I believe that counselling and psychotherapy should be available to them.

Their lives have generally got stressful and painful in certain specific ways that are part of the experience of becoming a refugee. This book seeks to outline those specific areas of difficulty and the way in which they might affect the victims and survivors. My purpose is to draw attention to those areas of experience which are likely to be significant for refugees seeking counselling. I do not wish for a moment to suggest that all people will experience the same events in the same way or that they will have the same reactions. I believe that one of the most important things to remember in counselling and psychotherapy is that individuals are individual, and while there are certain universal generalizations one might reasonably make about the human condition, the task of the counsellor or psychotherapist is precisely to discover the specific way in which one individual person deals with that universal condition.

Readers looking for diagnostic categories and labelled symptoms will be disappointed. I do not believe much in diagnosis except in the most vaguely general way of noting certain common aspects of lived experience, and I think it is more often a handicap than an aid to a constructive human encounter, which is what I take counselling and psychotherapy to be about.

I have used the term 'trauma' in the lay sense (as found in the Oxford English Dictionary) and I make no use of the concept of 'post-traumatic stress disorder' (PTSD). It is useful to be aware of the list of symptoms which constitute PTSD as they are experiences often presented by people who have suffered traumatic events. The nightmares, flashbacks, startle responses etc. are real enough. What is unhelpful is to regard them as some sort of medical syndrome to be treated and then cured, rather than as painful and distressing aspects of experience which have to be related to and understood.

The purpose of the torture and violence from which refugees have fled is, in the most part, to cow the population or inflict a political defeat, to impose political and/or cultural domination, to destroy the unity of oppositional communities, and to kill, wound and demoralize individuals in respect of their capacity to assert themselves politically and culturally. To medicalize their whole political, cultural, communal and existential suffering and their individual responses to this violent onslaught is to decontextualize it to the point where one risks undermining their struggle and contributing to the efforts of their persecutors. I offer this as a warning to those who seek the necessary professional detachment through psychological or medical diagnostic categories.

Detachment is important to be sure, but there are many ways to achieve it. Robert Lifton, in Caroline Garland's 'The Survivor Syndrome Workshop' (1980), has drawn on Martin Buber's concept of 'distance and relation' to emphasize the need for both detachment and engagement. Buber argues that it is only by setting oneself apart from another (at a distance) where one can experience oneself as separate from the other, that one can see clearly who that other is and relate properly to him or her – the 'I–thou' relationship. I hope that the framework offered in this book can contribute something to establishing a level of detachment from the refugee client's experience from which a human engagement is then possible.

It is this engagement that allows the therapist to bear witness to the client's experience. This bearing witness is a vital part of the therapeutic process. It involves the recognition and validation of the client's experience at all its different levels. This activity of recognizing, validating and struggling to make sense of violent, chaotic and disorientating experiences is the core of the work.

In this approach transference and regression are not encouraged. They are recognized and understood, but not regarded as therapeutic tools for 'working through'. Regression and dependency are to be recognized and addressed by enabling the client to mobilize adult ego functions to contain regressed feeling, and by being explicit about the limitations of the therapist's powers. The therapist therefore functions not as a parent figure but as a representative of human society, and of hope.

One further word of warning: because this is a book about the problem areas which refugees might need to talk about in counselling and psychotherapy it should not be seen as a contribution to a discourse that sees refugees as a bundle of needs to be met, or a population solely in need of looking after. While many may have profound needs, and may at an early stage in their settlement need a good deal of help, it should not be forgotten that they are also people with personal resources and talents capable of rebuilding their own lives and contributing to the society in which they have settled. Indeed counselling should, in my view, be seen not as a way of treating them so that they can then get on with their lives, but as a way of playing a small part in their project of creating *their* own future, which is also inextricably linked with *our* future. At least those of us with any sort of psychoanalytic or psychodynamic orientation should remember that Freud himself was a refugee.

CHAPTER 3

Assessment, Suitability and Adaptation

Questions are often raised as to how to assess the suitability of refugee clients for counselling or psychotherapy. The question tends to imply that counselling and psychotherapy are relatively constant and homogenous services for which individuals may be deemed suitable, or not.

To answer this question, I want to tell a short story. Some 30 years ago I was a researcher on a project developing youth work in what were described as 'multiracial areas'. The original idea was to discover how to run youth clubs in which white and black youths could mix. However, the emphasis of the project soon shifted its focus onto the specific needs that were being presented to the youth service by young black people. Concurrently, an effort was being made to recruit more black youth workers; so a number of black adults who had been helping out voluntarily at their local youth clubs were encouraged to go on youth and community work courses. Within a fairly short space of time, many of those people were saying to their tutors and course organizers, 'What you are teaching us does not relate to our experience of working with young black people. Your conception of "youth and community work" does not address the issues they present to us.'

It took a while for the significance of this message to be understood but eventually it became clear. If the youth service was going to engage meaningfully with young black people it was not going to be enough to simply provide more of what it had traditionally provided; i.e. encourage them to attend traditional youth clubs and provide an increased number of black youth leaders. What was actually going to be required was a rethinking of what was meant by youth and community work and what were the skills needed for doing it.

The situation is much the same for counselling and psychotherapy with refugees. We have to ask not 'Which clients are suitable for counselling or psychotherapy?', but 'How can we make our counselling and psychotherapy suitable for the clients?' This may mean rethinking what we mean by these terms 'counselling' and 'psychotherapy', rather than assuming we can do what we normally do with a few minor modifications.

Much is often made of the fact that counselling and psychotherapy do not exist in many of the societies from which refugees have come. What is less commonly observed is that most if not all cultures have some form of communication available for the expression of pain and distress. This often involves talking to someone else about one's experiences. It may also involve the use of dance, music or art or there may be other specific rituals.

Psychotherapists and counsellors have developed their skills in the art of communication. It is therefore the responsibility of the counsellor or psychotherapist to work out with the client what means of communication might best suit the client as a way of expressing what he or she needs to express.

In the specific case of talking therapies, the assessment question is simple. Does the client want to talk about his or her situation and experiences? If so, then the counsellor or psychotherapist is a person available to talk with. It is then up to the counsellor/psychotherapist to find a way of helping the client to talk about whatever it is that he or she needs to talk about.

Throughout this book I use the terms psychotherapy and counselling interchangeably. I do this because in my experience these terms refer not so much to specifically different practices but to different ways of labelling the practitioners according to which training course they have done. There is considerable overlap between training in psychotherapy and training in counselling. How one distinguishes one from the other, while it might feel initially important to the practitioners themselves, is of little relevance to the refugee client who has something important to communicate and is in search of someone to help him or her to communicate it.

This book offers a framework within which to work with refugee clients. Some of it is fairly familiar psychodynamic stuff. Other parts of it involve thinking in more unfamiliar ways and engaging with discourses outside the usual counselling and psychotherapy theory and practice. The challenge to counsellors and psychotherapists is therefore to adapt the skills and experience they already have and to learn some new skills and engage with some new experiences.

It is tempting at this point to embark on an exhaustive list of adaptations that might be made, but I do not think such a list is possible. I will therefore offer just one example.

Several of our counsellors at the Medical Foundation had clients who regularly missed appointments. Discussing this together we realized that the clients were effectively reducing the frequency of their sessions from once weekly. On further reflection, it occurred to us that this was as much as they could tolerate; remembering and revisiting painful experiences once a week was too much. They needed a longer recovery period and time to live in the present before they again revisited the traumatic past. When the counsellors began asking these clients if they would like to attend less frequently, the clients promptly confirmed our speculations and took up the offer. So we now have a number of clients who attend on a fortnightly, three-weekly, or four-weekly basis; and we have learned that counselling does not have to take place on the traditional weekly basis and that we need to allow our clients to guide us accordingly (see also Chapter 7).

Part II

The Refugee's Experience

CHAPTER 4

Political Level

Politics in the therapeutic context

When I first began working as a psychotherapist with refugees who were survivors of torture and organized violence I was told by a refugee colleague, 'Always remember, we are here because we lost!'

Refugees have become refugees because they have been losers (or sometimes innocent bystanders) or simply victims in a *political* conflict.

The political dimension of their experience is what has made them refugees. It is therefore, in many ways, the most significant determining factor in their current situation, yet it is the area most often neglected by psychotherapists and counsellors. Often the client's wish to talk about the political history of his or her country is regarded by the therapist as a defence or an avoidance rather than as a vitally important way of making sense of what has happened to the client, and recovering and rebuilding a sense of his or her own identity and place in the world.

Influenced by trainings that emphasize the importance of intrapsychic dynamics, individual behaviour or interpersonal communication, it may be a huge step for a therapist to take, to enter the world of politics. Even those trainings that consider culture and transcultural issues as important are seldom able to engage directly with the political world, its impact on personality development and its manifestation in and influence on the therapeutic encounter.

Psychotherapy is always a political activity because the construction of intersubjective meaning always has political implications and cannot escape ideological influences. However, this fact is generally ignored or denied within the psychotherapeutic discourse.

The client's political history

For refugees who have been political activists, their political activities and beliefs have usually been central to their identity. They therefore experience defeat and exile in a number of ways.

Where their political movements have been comprehensively defeated, perhaps to the point of annihilation, they can experience a profound loss of hope and a sense of futility. Their life's work has come to nothing and they have to face a future in which all the things they hoped for are no longer possible. It is not just their political movement that has been defeated. They themselves are defeated, and that may be the primary definition they have of themselves and their place in the world.

The sense of defeat may be accompanied by self-recrimination and self-doubt about the political movement itself, particularly about the wisdom of particular strategic and tactical decisions which the clients may have taken themselves or supported others in taking. There may also be self-condemnation and enormous shame and guilt if they have acted in any way that might have harmed the cause in general or specific people. If for example they have disclosed information under torture they may feel they have betrayed the movement, their friends and associates, and themselves.

Sometimes they may feel they have put their families in danger by being politically active. They then struggle with the conflict between their loyalty to their political movement (their own moral and ethical beliefs and convictions) and their loyalty to their families who would not otherwise have come to the attention of the security forces. It is not unusual for police or soldiers raiding a home in search of a political activist, and finding the activist not at home, to beat, arrest, torture, rape or kill whoever does happen to be there.

Some defeated political activists feel they have been betrayed by their own leaders. The leaders have taken the wrong decision, made the wrong alliances, or advanced their own interests at the expense of the movement. These betrayals may be by leaders in their home countries or by the leaders of the movement in exile. In either case the clients are likely to feel a profound sense of disillusionment and hopelessness, which may feel like a worse defeat than the one inflicted by their political opponents.

Politics in exile

Most refugees who have been politically active in their own countries are faced with a decision as to whether they resume political activity in exile. They may be disillusioned. They may feel they have had enough of politics. They may be frightened further by what has happened to them, or what might yet happen to their family members who are still in their home country. It is usually believed that there are informers in many if not most refugee communities, who can send word back to their government about the activities of opponents in exile.

Refugees must also struggle with the relationships of this country, in which they have sought refugee, with the regimes from which they have escaped. On the one hand they are grateful for being given a place of safety. On the other hand they may feel fiercely critical and deeply resentful of the political support, economic aid, arms and other military equipment that may have been supplied by our government to theirs.

Many refugees keep watch on the host country's* media coverage, or lack of it, of events in their own countries. When is the UK media interested? When is it not interested? To which side in the conflict is it sympathetic? How is their country and its people depicted? All of which adds up to: how well is their personal suffering understood? Who supports their cause? Who wants to hear their voice? Is there any justice? Or does media interest, and perhaps their therapist's political interest, reflect the political and economic interests of the UK, or the west, or big business?

When they see friendly relations developing between the UK and the regime they have escaped from, they feel not only betrayed at a political and moral level, but also anxious about their physical safety, since such a rapprochement might entail the UK government declaring their country of origin a safe place for asylum seekers to go back to and consequently turning down their application.

It is important to remember that refugees who have obtained full refugee status are relatively rare. Most have some sort of conditional permission to stay in the UK or are in the process of applying for asylum or appealing against its refusal.

---

*   Host country is the most convenient term we can find, but it needs to be recognized that the host country may be rather inhospitable.

The significance of politics

I have referred earlier to 'political activists', but it would be a mistake to assume that it is only to such activists that these issues apply.

First, the distinction between activists and non-activists is different in English society from many other parts of the world. In England there are activists who are passionately committed to political causes; then there are those who may support a party or cause, without being very actively involved; and there are non-activists who take a rather detached and perhaps cynical view of politics, regarding all politicians with suspicion, feeling somewhat indifferent with regard to which party wins an election and feeling that none of it has a great deal of impact on their own lives. In other parts of the world the majority of the population often feel far more invested in political parties or movements, and their lives are much more profoundly influenced by who is in power, whether or not there are elections, whether there is a coup and whether there is freedom of speech or assembly. A change in government may mean they become subject to persecution or discrimination just because of their tribal identity, religion, class position, cultural or ethnic tradition, or domicile in an area that is a stronghold of the previous ruling party.

In poor countries that have gone through long periods of political turmoil, people may have high hopes that certain leaders or movements can alleviate these situations. So even if they are not personally active in the political arena they are psychologically invested in the political process.

Colonial and post-colonial relationships

Many refugees come from countries that have been colonized and they are acutely aware of the colonial history, the post-colonial relationship, and the way in which the persecution they have suffered can be understood in the context of that long historical relationship.

Members of post-colonial societies are invariably profoundly influenced by the colonial legacy. The language they speak will often be that of the colonizer. Their religion may be that brought by missionaries from the colonial power. Their education system may have been modelled on that of the colonizer and they may have been taught by English or European teachers.

Members of these societies will probably not have encountered white people who do not occupy positions of power and authority. They therefore bring a set of conscious or unconscious assumptions about the relative status of white Anglo/European/Western people and themselves, and a sort of socio-political transference which will be present in the therapeutic encounter. Indeed, the whole colonial and post-colonial history is, in some sense, going to be there in the therapy room.

For some refugees, the former colonial power is idealized. They have high expectations about the levels of wealth, opportunity, freedom, democracy and tolerance they will find. They are shocked by the culture of scepticism and hostility to asylum seekers, the casual racism of many institutions and sectors of society and the levels of poverty and deprivation among the indigenous population. Most refugees, except those who manage to bring money out of their own countries, find that in the host country they are members of an underclass that they never knew existed in societies like ours.

The location of the therapist in the client's political context

In all of this the position of the therapist is always implicitly in question. In my view all psychotherapy is a political activity, and the idea of therapeutic neutrality is inherently problematic. While it is possible to be neutral about certain issues, it is not possible in a political, social, cultural and moral context to be completely neutral. One cannot *not* have a gender, a cultural identity, a class position, a moral position or set of beliefs, and importantly a belief in a particular model of therapy (and modes of therapy usually imply significant beliefs about the human condition), all of which have political and ideological implications. It is therefore important for therapists to have some understanding of their own political position and beliefs while recognizing that they will be unconscious of much of the political significance of their position and approach. And it is important to recognize that the client will have conscious and unconscious fantasies/phantasies* and anxieties about the therapist's political position (see Chapter 8).

For example: I once took four clients whom I had been seeing individually and brought them together into a group. One of the first things they discussed in the group was their shared experience of all coming from different countries that Britain had colonized. In several sessions of individual therapy, none of them had made any reference at all to colonialism. It was only the safety of numbers that enabled them to raise an issue about which I might have taken offence. Indeed there are few clients who will risk expressing angry or critical feelings about the host country or its government without

---

*   For readers unfamiliar with this distinction: 'fantasy' is conscious, 'phantasy' is unconscious.

some indication from the therapist that he or she will not be unsympathetic to such views.

The location of the therapist's agency in the client's political context

The therapist's agency will also have a place in the overall social and political structure. This is something for the therapist to think about and be aware of. It is also something about which the clients will have perception and beliefs. For example, is the therapist's agency connected to the Home Office? Is it a statutory agency? Is it a human rights organization? What is its position in relation to the refugee community? What is its position in relation to human rights?

CHAPTER 5

Cultural Level

Cultural transition

The reality of the refugee position is that it is one of cultural transition. Refugees do not occupy one culture. They occupy at least two: the one they left and the one they have arrived in.

The state of transition, moreover, is not one they are going to pass through. It is one they are going to live with. There will be no time in their lives when they will be able to have not come from the country they left. And there will be no point in their lives when they will be able to return to their country and rejoin the culture they left because it will not be the same culture they left; and they, having lived in a different culture, will not be the same people.

In the modern world, with so much more geographical and social mobility and so much interpenetration between cultures, the condition of cultural transition is one in which many people live. There is also a condition of multiculturality whereby an individual can participate in or be a member of a number of unrelated cultures in which he or she can, in effect, have different identities in different social settings.

However, these cultural transitions and multicultural identities involve varying degrees of choice. For refugees the degree of choice is minimal and because of the circumstances of the transition, the transitional state may be particularly acute and its contradictions may be particularly sharp.

Refugee clients may present issues of culture in a sharply defined way. They may also cling to aspects of the culture from which they have been separated in a particularly tenacious way. This may involve freezing in their minds their own culture at the time they left it and failing to acknowledge how it might have evolved. So they remain loyal to a culture in their mind that no longer exists in the contemporary reality, but only in historical reality.

A symbolic universe

A culture is the symbolic universe of its members. It is the matrix of representation, enactment, communication and meaning through which people collectively manage the conflicts of their individual inner worlds, the conflicts between the needs and desires of the individual and those of the collective, and the conflicts between individuals and between different interest groups within the total collective body.

All societies must manage the basics of biological survival – feeding, defecating and sexual reproduction – and the emotions that emanate from these processes. And, in order to function as societies, they must organize social units for the nurturing and care of children; for cooperative activities, between members, for the management of hostilities and rivalries; and for the generation of the systems of shared meaning and communication which are essential for cooperative activity. Culture is the organization of collective human life and, indeed, of the meaning of life. And these meanings are internalized in the individual ego or self.

Culture not only involves a way of organizing life and its meanings (through rules and procedures and institutions), but also ways of dramatizing and reflecting on the issues of life and death and meaning in that society. Thus there is music, sport, dance, drama, literature, poetry, story telling and humour in most if not all societies, all of which embody, enact, refract and reflect upon the systems of value, status and meaning, and upon fundamental existential themes of life, death, love, hate, romance, tragedy, violence, destruction, betrayal, revenge, success, failure, triumph, defeat, loss, change, competition, cooperation etc.

All these are issues that a society must address collectively and that the individual must also resolve in him or herself. Culture is thus part of the outer world internalized in the individual and the individual world externalized in the society.

Any cultural transition therefore involves not only a change in an individual's relationship with something external, but also a reorganization of the internal world, the internal symbolic universe which corresponds to the external symbolic universe we usually call culture. So, therapy that seeks to address cultural issues or cultural transition is not focusing on something external, but on the internal structuring of individual mental life.

Cultural complexity and evolution

A great deal of polemic has been written and talked about culture. Culture is often presented as some ossified monolithic entity. A statement prefaced 'In my culture we...' becomes hallowed, incontrovertible and non-negotiable. In this formulation culture is some sort of pristine form of collective harmony unchanging over time, unsullied by politics and economics, providing traditional solutions to all problems, and a constant source of sustenance and support for all its members.

This sort of 'culture' is perceived as a positive part of an individual's life and something that has been sullied or contaminated by the repressive government, western imperialism, and exile in an alien environment. The only times the word culture is used pejoratively is when it is used to refer to 'western culture' which is usually the villain of the piece having failed to recognize the validity of any value system other than its own such as 'eastern culture' or 'indigenous cultures'.

In this scenario, refugees and other migrants are often depicted as being shoehorned into inappropriate categories by 'western medicine' or 'western psychology' which fails to understand and respect their 'culture'.

The problem with all this is not that it does not have a significant degree of truth and relevance, but it readily becomes such a gross oversimplification that it obfuscates as much as it reveals and militates against meaningful transcultural negotiation. It is true for example that the evolution of many cultures in what we now call 'third world' societies was interrupted, diverted and to some extent forestalled by colonization. Many of those traditions have survived and developed in spite of colonization and continue to have a distinctively different if not oppositional set of values and beliefs to those of the colonizing power. Some of these traditions have however been virtually destroyed. It is also true that many western governments, and professionals, and to some extent the cultures of western societies fail to recognize the validity of any value system other than their own. But then not many cultures do recognize the validity of value systems other than their own. And one could argue that 'western medicine' and 'western psychology' have trouble recognizing and understanding *any* culture, including their *own*!

Cultural imperialism is a continuing phenomenon. It remains a danger when therapeutic models derived from one culture are applied in work with people from a different culture. However, if the problem is to be realistically addressed its complexity and uncertainty have to be recognized and respected.

First, virtually no culture is static. This was a mistake made by early anthropologists who thought the 'traditional societies' they studied had always been and would continue to be as they found them. In fact cultures evolve, and at any given time are therefore in a state of change.

Second, cultures have internal conflicts. Indeed their evolution frequently proceeds through a conflict between those who want change and those who want to keep things as they are. Conflicts between generations and between genders are common. Tensions have existed between young and older generations in many societies throughout history, and today there are few societies that do not have a feminist movement challenging traditional gender roles.

Third, cultures are not hermetically sealed. They are penetrated by other cultures. In the colonial era, traditional cultures or particular aspects of them were often kept alive alongside the imposed culture of the colonizer. In the current era of globalization, western investments and products (Nike, Levi's, McDonald's, Coca-Cola) are ubiquitous. Often these influences create their own tensions and conflicts with the existing culture and these tensions may dovetail with a country's internal political conflicts, tensions between generations or other pre-existing fault lines.

Fourth, societies do not have only one culture, they have numerous subcultures. There are different social classes and different geographical areas, each with their own subcultures and dialects, as well as the commonly found differences between urban and rural cultures.

Fifth, cultures are not only self-referential – that is to say, they do not only embody beliefs, values and meanings referring to the members of that culture; they also bear assumptions, beliefs, myths and attitudes to *other* cultures. They may be deferential or hostile, or both, towards the colonial power. They may assume superiority over neighbouring societies. Cultures thus organize not only the way in which their members relate to each other, but also the way their members relate to the members of other cultures.

Migrants who feel somewhat at sea in an alien culture are apt to cling more vigorously to their own culture and to remember it in a particularly positive, simplified and uncritical way. They resist entering the state of transition with its divided loyalties, conflicts and threats to identity. Instead they recall their own cultures with the passion of a lover, and cling to beliefs and practices that may have been of less significance to them had they still been in their home country. Similarly they may forget many of the negative aspects of their culture, the things they were critical of or felt themselves personally inhibited by or in conflict with. Indeed it may have been their conflict with some aspects of that culture that led to them being persecuted and driven into exile, but they may not feel ready to see it in those terms.

There may well be good reason for hanging onto their culture in this way. They may be in a continuing state of shock or psychic numbing (see Chapter 7), having witnessed or survived horrifying events. It may be that clinging to their culture is the only way available to them to hold themselves together, provide their lives with some sort of continuity and meaning and maintain some sense of who they are. A language they cannot speak and a hostile reception from the local community do little to assist them in moving towards a sense of transition.

Moving into a state of transition can only be done at one's own speed. In families, this may be a particular source of conflict as some family members move into the transitional state more rapidly than others. Children often learn the language of the host society much more quickly than their parents. Women may find they are offered opportunities and freedoms that were not available to them previously while men may find themselves unable to work and earn the status they have been used to, and unable to command the same level of authority and respect simply by virtue of being men.

CHAPTER 6

Interpersonal Level

Loss and separation

Immediate family, extended family, friends and colleagues provide a major dimension of personal identity. They are, in many ways, the mainstays of an individual's existence: the context within which his or her sense of self is formed and maintained.

Nearly all refugees will have suffered losses in this area. Many will have had family, friends and colleagues killed. Often they have witnessed the killings or they may have been away at work or school and returned home to find the bodies. Others may have been miles away and received news of the death, days, weeks or months later. They may never have seen the bodies and have had no chance to bury them – which in some cultures can be a devastating omission. Some feel that members of their family have been killed because of what they themselves have done politically. Or perhaps they feel guilty just because they were unable to protect their families. Sometimes, so many friends and family members have been killed that the survivors seem unable to begin any sort of mourning process and appear on the surface to be relatively unmoved. Such presentations can often obscure the depth of grief which can take many months or even years to emerge.

In other cases, family and friends may have been 'lost' in the sense that they have been left behind, or have fled to another country. Sometimes they are still in communication by phone or letter, but often contact has been lost and there is little realistic expectation that they will ever meet again. These losses too may be spoken of in a relatively matter-of-fact sort of way which can obscure the degree to which they are actually felt.

Family and friends left behind may still be in danger. Attempts to contact them might increase the danger, particularly where phone calls are monitored or mail interfered with. Sometimes they are simply missing and there is no way of knowing whether they are alive or dead, but attempts to find out might increase the possibility of them ending up dead. The refugees then have to live with an abiding and growing anxiety which they sometimes feel acutely and are sometimes cut off from completely. Friends and family in the home country often assume that once a refugee has 'made it to the west' he or she will have access to money and influence, so they write or telephone asking for money to be sent for various pressing needs or for political activities to be undertaken. The recipients of such requests may feel a considerable sense of failure and shame that they are not able to respond as they would wish. They do not know how to begin explaining the realities of their predicament in exile.

Some refugees who have fled without their families may subsequently regret having left them behind. It may be extremely hard in such circumstances to come to terms with the fact that they were so terrified and desperate to escape that they fled without thinking what would happen to their families or how they were going to be reunited. In some cases flight may have been the only realistic alternative to their own death. Nevertheless, the feeling that they should have stayed anyway, irrational though it may be, can still lurk in the back of their minds, or even in the front, or it may be completely repressed.

The family in exile

The violence refugees have suffered and the events they have survived may have a profound effect on relationships between family members. Children may be profoundly affected by seeing their parents beaten and humiliated and particularly by seeing their mothers raped or knowing that this has happened.

Rape and other forms of torture can create a barrier between adult sexual partners. It can feel as if the torturers or rapists have inserted themselves between the couple. Where victims are unable to tell their partner what has been done to them, they can feel left with a secret which they share only with the torturer and not with their partner.

Furthermore, the victim may be significantly transformed by the experience. A happy, confident person may become timid and frightened, or paranoid and explosively angry, or depressed and withdrawn. Parents who have enjoyed being with their children and have managed them confidently can become unable to stand their children's noise and boisterousness, either withdrawing physically and emotionally, or becoming angry and even violent at the least provocation. Such situations are perplexing and frightening to the children, the spouse and to the parent him or herself who is unable to recognize or make sense of his or her own behaviour. Few experiences are as disorientating as having a family member change almost overnight into someone unrecognizable as the parent or spouse one has always known. But it can be even worse to discover that one has oneself changed into someone different from the person one always knew oneself to be, and that one is not only unable to relate to one's loved ones in the way one has always done, but finds oneself instead behaving towards them in a frightening, hostile and rejecting way that one would not previously have believed possible.

Conflicts of loyalty and feelings of shame, guilt and betrayal may play a major part in interpersonal relationships. Wives may resent husbands for having pursued political activities they knew to be dangerous. The wife may even have warned the husband and asked him to stop. Subsequently she may blame him for the suffering brought on the rest of the family as a result of his activities. This may include the deaths of other family members or just the fact that the family has been forced into exile with all its consequences. Such resentments can be harboured in silence behind a veil of apparent cooperation, compliance and support, or they may be more openly expressed.

The activist may in turn feel resentful at the lack of wholehearted support, or lack of understanding of the importance of the struggle in which he or she has been involved. Some activists feel a huge burden of responsibility and guilt for what they have put their family through. This feeling is often compounded in the situation of exile where they are unable to work and thereby to look after their family.

The situation of exile in a different culture can put additional stresses on interpersonal relationships. Conflicts can develop within families between those who find aspects of the new culture attractive and those who cling to the traditions of their homeland. Most obviously women may find and seize the opportunity to be less subordinated to their husbands and to men in general, and children may claim the new freedoms from parental and adult authority. These women and children may also feel internally conflicted between joining in the new culture and making new friends in the host society and remaining loyal to their families and refugee communities.

The client and therapist

In this context the client's relationship with the therapist becomes vitally important. The therapist may be the one person the client feels able to trust and talk to. Family members have to be protected from the awful memories and feelings. Those outside the family might not be trustworthy whether they are from the homeland or from the new host community.

The therapist may also be experienced as having all the necessary knowledge the client needs, and all the necessary authority and influence to sort out problems with the Home Office, the housing department, the children's school, the GP etc. There is some truth in this, for the therapist does indeed have a great deal of knowledge and influence compared to the client, and may well be able to exercise this on the client's behalf. The therapist has to decide how much of this sort of work to do (see Chapter 13), and at the same time recognize the effect that it has on the relationship with the client.

More importantly, the therapist is a witness. Refugees often need to tell their story, to be believed, and to have someone share their shock and horror at what has happened to them. Otherwise they remain anonymous: nameless and faceless casualties of a war or persecution that few people have heard of and even fewer know anything about. Even those refugees from highly publicized conflicts can feel like mere statistics, or pictures on a television screen. So the role of the therapist as witness becomes vitally important. The therapist is a witness not just to the history of a particular conflict, but to the client's particular lived experience of the conflict. The political and the personal are thus brought together in that act of witnessing. A client may subsequently wish to move from the interpersonal back to the political by giving his or her 'testimony' to a human rights organization such as Amnesty International to contribute to the body of evidence of human rights violations by the regime from which he or she has escaped.

CHAPTER 7

Intrapsychic Level

Violence and terror

Not all refugees have been directly exposed to extreme levels of violence, terror and destruction, but since it is essentially from violence and persecution that they have sought refuge, there will be few who have been untouched by it. Its impact will therefore be present to varying degrees in the minds of those seeking help.

Exposure to extreme levels of violence, terror and destruction stirs up the most primitive feelings and anxieties, to a degree where many people's normal defensive structures are unable to cope. They may experience a sense of being overwhelmed or of drowning in their feelings. As human beings themselves, it may be impossible for them to reconcile their own sense of humanity with the violence and destructiveness they have witnessed and encountered in their fellow humans. Their own feelings of rage, hatred, anger and destructiveness can become unmanageable or even impossible to contemplate. Indeed the whole experience can become simply too much to think about in any coherent way. In some situations the confident expectation of death, or overwhelming feelings of fear and anxiety, not only for their own survival but in relation to the sheer scale and violence of the onslaught, are just too much to manage.

Although it seems to be suggested in some of the literature that responses to *trauma* do not differ significantly according to the actual nature of the trauma, this is just not true in our experience. The fact that the trauma is not a natural disaster, nor an unintended accident, but is intentionally contrived and deliberately inflicted – an act of human will – is of considerable significance, not least in the way it makes it hard for victims to comprehend how such things could be done.

Moreover, in situations of mass violence and persecution, individuality is rendered totally insignificant. The erstwhile individual person disappears into a merged persecutory context. He or she ceases to exist. There are, therefore, in psychoanalytic terms, high levels of anxiety related to annihilation, engulfment, disintegration and destructiveness.

Where individuals have been singled out for persecution because of their political activities, and also in many cases of more general purges and state repressions aimed at whole populations, the intention of the repressive regime is to destroy the potency of its opponents. The aim of the violence is therefore to metaphorically castrate the opposition, or the minority group: to disempower them. Consequently castration anxieties and libidinal inhibitions are also greatly intensified. Even where the refugees have not directly suffered traumatic violence to themselves or their families, the whole experience of exile may produce a powerful sense of abandonment, helplessness and diminished potency and competence.

Psychic numbing

The common response to overwhelming feelings and anxieties in the face of overwhelming violence, and in the face of complex (and often incomprehensible) political processes, is to go numb: to feel nothing, and to be largely unable to think.

The term 'psychic numbing' was coined by Robert Lifton in his *Death in Life – Survivors of Hiroshima* (1968) to describe the state of atomic bomb survivors whose first reaction to the annihilations of Hiroshima and Nagasaki was to sit in stunned disbelief: unable to respond at all, seemingly unable even to begin to take in the enormity of what had happened.

Many traumatized refugees exhibit this sort of numbing in various forms and to varying degrees. Often in order to survive and escape, they have got certain parts of themselves to function, while other parts have gone into some sort of shock and shut down. In other cases they seem to have functioned effectively in dealing with the immediate situations with which they were faced in order to make the flight into exile (and perhaps to deal with some of the basic requirements of resettlement) and then to have gone into a sort of delayed shock in which they are unable to remember clearly what has happened, are unable to think or talk about it, and unable to experience any emotional response to it.

Fragmentation

As the shock and numbing subside, memories, thoughts and feelings begin to emerge in a disjoined and fragmented way. Stories begin to emerge as bits and pieces of events whose connection or sequence can be quite unclear. (Presumably it is precisely this disconnectedness and apparent inconsistency that can lead immigration officials to doubt the veracity of many of the accounts given by asylum seekers.)

The symptoms listed as constituents of PTSD can be understood as fragments of experiences: nightmares, flash-backs, startle reactions, hypervigilance etc. – pieces of a jigsaw which need to be connected and translated into a coherent story. This fragmented communication reflects, in my view, a fragmented internal state in which aspects of context and identity, experience and history, value and meaning cannot be connected. Time and space can also become fragmented, and attendance at appointments can become apparently quite haphazard. Missed appointments or arrivals ten minutes before the end of a session are not at all uncommon. These reflect, I believe, both an internal state of fragmentation and disorganization and an internal unconscious organization which chooses to limit the amount of therapeutic contact time which can in itself be overwhelming.

The need to remember and the wish to forget

A former Medical Foundation colleague, Andrea Sabbadini referred to the need to remember and the wish to forget to sum up the two powerful forces he encountered as internal conflicts for his clients.

As the memories and feelings begin to take shape they bring with them acute anxieties and potentially overwhelming levels of grief, rage and horror – the feelings that have been kept at bay by the numbing and the fragmentation. It is at this point that the client in counselling/psychotherapy becomes aware both of a powerful wish to put the past behind him or her and think positively about the future, and of a need to recognize and integrate his or her own experiential history in order to recover a sense of historical self which can effectively engage with the future.

It is at this point that it is worth thinking from a therapeutic point of view about the frequency of sessions. The client needs to live sufficiently in the present in order to feel secure and grounded enough to be able to revisit a horrifying past, without being overwhelmed by it. The client is struggling to prevent the past from overwhelming the present and future, so the relative amount of time spent in the two different places needs to be regulated. One therapy hour per week, i.e. one visit per week into the past, may not allow a sufficient recovery time in the present. Fortnightly, three-weekly, monthly or even more infrequent sessions may therefore need to be considered. As already noted in Chapter 3, clients not offered this option often vote with their feet by missing appointments.

Jorge Semprun, a former prisoner from Buchenwald, described many years later how sometimes it seemed that Buchenwald had been a nightmare and his present life was reality, and at other times it seemed that Buchenwald was the reality and his current life was a dream. Many survivors have a similar experience of the discontinuity between their present context in which they now live and horrific past experiences that they are trying to come to terms with. To talk too little of the past allows it to assume the status of a nightmare that could not really have happened, or perhaps happened to someone else. But to talk too much about it, to visit it and re-experience parts of it too frequently can loosen one's grip on current reality and distort the person's contemporary sense of identity and place in the world.

The adult and the infant

So overwhelming are the experiences of some refugee clients that they may appear to have regressed to infantile levels of helplessness and dependency, and they may indeed experience themselves and their overwhelming feelings in this way. The effect of their experience has been to undermine and at times annihilate their adult capacity to take a place in the world, manage a part of the world, cope with powerful feelings, manage difficult situations, learn from experience etc., yet it is precisely that part of themselves (the adult ego in psycho-dynamic terms) that is most needed to begin to think about and contain the chaotic fragments of experience and emotion with which they are struggling.

It has been said that in 'trauma' the internal mother is a by-standing observer. Many traumatized refugees present them-selves in a state which suggests that the internal mother who contains and organizes the chaotic experience of the infant has indeed been removed from their psychic structure. However, it is a mistake to regard this simply as regression, and such a mistake may lead the unwary counsellor to further undermine the functioning adult capacities of the client by failing to recognize them, adopting an overprotective position and treat-ing the client as unduly fragile.

The adult ego has in fact survived the experiences at some level, and has reached a place of exile and provisional safety where it continues to function. Most importantly, it continues to function in struggling to manage and make sense of the experiences it has survived and which it continues to survive.

The importance of recognizing and addressing the 'adult-who-feels-like-an-infant' and not addressing oneself to an 'infant-who-looks-like-an-adult' or the 'infant-whom-the-adult-feels-like' cannot be overemphasized.

Victim and survivor

In a split not dissimilar to the one described above, between adult and infant, a client can present him or herself either as victim or survivor, in such a way that one identity seems to preclude the other – whereas, in fact, they inhabit both identities.

As victims they experience themselves and present themselves as relatively helpless: overwhelmed by symptoms, feelings and unmanageable problems; unable to get to appointments on time; unable to walk two miles to get to an appointment despite having no physical injuries; unable to talk to school teachers about their children and their education or to negotiate with other officials or institutions. At these times the person who has carried out the often complex and demanding task of surviving and escaping from persecution and embarking on a new life in a new country seems to have completely disappeared.

The converse experience and presentation of the survivor is of being resilient and capable, undaunted by the problems of the present and unscarred by the experiences of the past. The experience of being a victim is banished, dissociated, split off or denied, and the possibility of acknowledging or revisiting that experience is regarded as dangerously threatening to the coping capacity so much in evidence.

Faced with these split presentations, the psychotherapist/counsellor has the task of reminding the 'victim' that he or she is also a 'survivor' and helping the 'survivor' come to terms with the fact that he or she has also been a 'victim' and is in some ways still carrying the scars and perhaps even bleeding from the wounds.

Survivor guilt

This is another term coined by Lifton to describe the feelings of guilt about having survived when others have not. This feeling is exacerbated in cases where the survivor has actually made compromises or concessions. Those who have given away information or signed confessions or renunciations of their beliefs, under torture or threat of death, feel acute guilt –

though paradoxically they do at least have a concrete act to which they can ascribe their guilt, while those who have simply survived without any sort of concession or compromise can be haunted by a far less readily explicable but nevertheless persistent and insidious sense of guilt about the mere fact of them still being alive. Others may have complex unconscious feelings about having escaped, leaving others behind. In cases where spouses and children have been left, it may be far more possible, however painful, to be conscious of missing those people acutely than it is to access doubt, self-reproach or guilt at having left them. Revisiting the moments of decision at the point of flight involve revisiting the terror that instigated the flight. It therefore needs to be approached only with great caution and sensitivity.

Overwhelming rage

Anger and rage are often the emotions that most threaten to overwhelm the victim/survivor. Frequently they become excessively passive, accommodating and grateful for the smallest things in order to avoid the possibility of confrontation or conflict which would trigger an anger which will almost immediately become an uncontrollable rage.

Parents, particularly fathers, can find themselves so un-settled by the minor irritations, noise or general boisterousness of their children that they have to withdraw into a room on their own or go out of the living space in order to calm themselves down. Others can find themselves unaccountably exploding or lashing out over the most minor provocations.

Much of this is connected to the breakdown of the internal capacity for containment and self-control inflicted by torture and violence already referred to. However, it also seems that being the victim of such persecution generates an urge to disidentify and distinguish oneself from the persecutor – an urge to claim the moral high ground for oneself and to preserve one's humanity by categorizing the persecutors as not properly members of the human race. To be in touch with one's own feelings of rage, violence, destructiveness and longing for revenge is to implicitly close that gap and to recognize in oneself some of the characteristics of the persecutor. Such a convergence can be a profoundly identity-threatening occurrence which has to be defended against through high levels of repression, denial and projection.

Shame

It is a striking fact that the shame, which might appropriately be felt by the perpetrators of injustice, torture, violence and genocide, is much more commonly borne by the victim.

Shame can be particularly powerful where refugees have suffered rape or other forms of sexual torture. Shame may also be mixed up with guilt over having survived, and what the person might have done in order to survive.

There are also more basic, primitive unconscious mechanisms whereby people can be ashamed of their bodies, their vulnerability, their helplessness and even their ill luck and need for help. The strength of this shame may prevent the client from even thinking about the sources of the shame. Furthermmore, although shame is felt internally it is also an interpersonal experience. It is particularly activated in trying to tell another person (such as a therapist) what has happened. My colleague, Dr Gill Hinshelwood, considers that this shame, or the repression and denial of it, may well be what most prevents the whole experience from being talked about. It can thus become the gatekeeping emotion which blocks access to other aspects of the experience in the therapeutic setting.

Part III
The Therapist's Experience

CHAPTER 8

Political Level

The therapist's political position

Therapy with political refugees implicitly questions the therapist's own political position. From what country does the therapist come? Is he or she from the host country? If so, how identified is the therapist with that government's asylum policy? How free and safe can the client feel in expressing both sides of his or her ambivalence – gratitude at being provided with a safe haven, anger at the disbelief and insensitivity he or she may have encountered through application, detention, voucher systems, dispersal etc?

What is the relationship of the host nation to the regime from which the client has escaped? Does it lend economic or military support to that regime, or has it done so in the past? Is the client's country politically or economically dominated by the host country? What does the therapist think and feel about these relationships?

If not from the host nation, where is the therapist from? Is the therapist from another western country that had colonies in the 'third world', or from the third world? Or perhaps from eastern Europe? How does the therapist then experience his or her relationship to the host country, and how identified is he or she with other third world people? Does the therapist have something in common with the client by coming from the same continent or geopolitical region? Or are the politics of the therapist's country largely disconnected from those of the client's home?

What is the therapist's political identity, party membership, class origins, voting habits? What is his or her analysis or understanding of colonization and post-colonization? What is his or her position on the host country's immigration and asylum policy?

The therapist here has two tasks, or perhaps one should say more realistically, *at least* two tasks: first, to recognize the ways in which the client may perceive their relative geopolitical locations and the sorts of significance the client may attach to this aspect of their relationship; second, to consider the therapist's own perception of this relationship, how he or she feels about it, and how it might affect his or her response to the client.

Some therapists, for example, may feel embarrassed or ashamed about their own government's asylum policy, or about its foreign policy, or about the racism and prejudice refugees encounter, or about the existence in their affluent society of a socio-economic underclass in which many refugees find themselves more or less automatically located. These are understandable feelings, and if they are understood and contained, they may contribute to the therapist's understanding of the client. They may even be talked about openly with the client, which may help develop the therapeutic relationships.

If however such feelings are avoided, split off, denied or repressed, or simply not contained, they may lead to the therapist becoming overprotective or overidentified with the client, or over-responsible for the client's predicament in an effort to compensate for the injustice. Or it may lead to the therapist unconsciously wishing to avoid discussing the client's concerns about the host country's government, and consequently blocking the client's attempts to raise such matters or subtly steering the therapeutic discussion in a different direction. Clients can, as we know, be acutely sensitive to their therapist's conscious and unconscious concerns and can rapidly unconsciously (and even consciously) discern what topics their therapists are not comfortable with.

Some therapists may themselves be, or have been, politically active. They may find their own political beliefs correspond closely with or diverge sharply from those of their clients. In such cases it is easy to perceive the client as a political ally or opponent. Again the crucial factor is the therapist's recognition of such situations and of the feelings involved. There is little point trying to pretend that such alliances or oppositions do not exist. What is important is for the therapist to monitor his or her feelings and to be aware of how they might be affecting the therapy.

Neutrality and the apolitical therapist

There are, no doubt, those who believe it is possible to be apolitical, or politically neutral, as a therapist. I do not believe this is possible.

It may be possible to strive towards operating in an even-handed and politically impartial way, but I doubt that it is possible to have no political thoughts, no feelings about political realities. This is not a question of party politics but rather about the way in which, for example, if one says the word 'communism', most people have a reaction to it; they have thoughts, feelings, associations, and understandings of what it means – and similarly if one says the words 'democracy', 'free speech' or 'class'.

The problem occurs when therapists, striving with the best will in the world to achieve the sublime state of therapeutic and political neutrality, deny that they have their own specific response to these terms, ideas and movements, and fail to recognize how such responses and understandings can affect their work as therapists, particularly in working with clients whose experience is so essentially political. It is then that the therapeutic process can become unconsciously skewed in a way that is difficult to deal with, precisely because it is unconscious. It is therefore the therapists' self-conscious awareness of their own politics that protects the therapy from such unconscious influence, rather than the belief that some mythical state of political neutrality is attainable and sustainable.

The therapist's knowledge (or ignorance) of the client's political context

Working with refugees from different parts of the world, it is clearly unrealistic to expect therapists to have detailed knowledge of all the different political situations from which they have fled. Indeed, in many situations the therapist may know little or nothing about the client's home country.

Where the therapist knows a good deal about the client's country there may still be a problem if the therapist thinks his or her knowledge is more detailed or more insightful than it actually is, or if he or she has a view of that country opposed to that of the client. Few people appreciate being told about the working of their own country by a foreigner.

It is always useful to have some background knowledge of the client's homeland's politics and political history. This may be gleaned from newspapers, books etc. Amnesty International are usually able to supply background information about most countries.

However, the most important source of information is usually the client him or herself. Refugee clients often need to talk at some length about the political complexities that have led to their persecution as part of the process of making sense of their experience. If the therapist is interested in listening to and understanding these explanations and prepared to ask about details he or she does not know about or understand, then the client has the sort of audience he or she needs. It will not matter that the therapist knows very little because it will give the client more opportunity to explain.

CHAPTER 9

Cultural Level

Culture as a looking glass

Over ten years ago, the Group Analytic Society (a European professional society) began a series of transcultural workshops in order to explore the different cultures and intercultural relationships embodied within the Society using the techniques of group analysis. One of the more remarkable conclusions from these workshops was that in one's encounters with other cultures, the thing one was most likely to learn was something about one's *own* culture. The things one had previously taken for granted as universals (because one never had cause to question them) were revealed, in encounters with other cultures which did not share them, to be not universals but culturally specific.

This is perhaps the most important experience for therapists working with refugees: the awareness and continuing discovery of their own culture through their encounters with people from other cultures.

One's own culture is also the best place to start from in setting out to understand someone from a different culture. It is quite impossible for any one person (particularly one working as a therapist and not as an anthropologist or sociologist) to know a great deal about a lot of other cultures. One can, however, have done sufficient work in thinking about and understanding one's own culture to begin the work of comparing it with and relating it to a different culture. One can also in this way begin to appreciate the importance of culture, the way it shapes our experience of ourselves and our world, and the difficulties that might be involved in leaving it and trying to live in another culture.

It is particularly important to recognize how much of what we think and believe is culturally relative, and belongs not to some sort of category of universals but to our own very specific culture or subculture. Psychotherapists and counsellors generally belong to a very specific professional middle-class subculture, which may be quite different from the wider society. For example, I have often heard it said that refugees come from a culture where they don't have counselling or psychotherapy so they don't know what it is. But I too grew up in a culture where they did not have counselling or psychotherapy, and had I not stumbled into the business, I would not have known what it was. That was in a provincial English city! Although in the UK nowadays most people have heard the term 'counselling', there are not that many who actually know what it means.

Similarly I have heard discussions about the subordinate place of women in the societies that some refugees come from, which seem to imply that 'our' society is some sort of paradigm of post-feminist gender equality. Whether 'our society' in these discussions is the whole of our country, our cosmopolitan cities, or the predominantly white, liberal, middle-class, intellectual community of psychotherapists and counsellors is never altogether clear.

Yet another example can be found in discussions about cultures where men allegedly do not express their feelings. No-one listening to such discussions would ever guess in which society the virtue of 'keeping a stiff upper lip' was first established – nor would they guess the extent to which it is still practised in various subcultures of that society.

So, we might safely say that the more we know about our own culture, the less vulnerable we are to simplistic myths and projections about other cultures.

This is also applicable to our understanding of the concept of culture itself. Thinking about our own culture, or cultures, enables us to recognize the dynamic nature of culture: the way it changes from one generation to the next, some traditions living on, others transformed, and yet others lost. We can see also that there are huge differences, conflicts and inconsistencies within cultures, and radically different interpretations of religious texts, artistic and literary traditions and political ideologies. Refugees, cut off from their culture and desperate to retain some cultural identity, often talk about culture as if it is some rigid monolithic and unchangeable thing. While it may be true that there are powerful and more or less constant traditions or traditional themes in their particular culture, and while they themselves may need to cling steadfastly to these themes, it is nevertheless important for the therapist to retain a wider perspective of the overall complexity, diversity and evolving dynamics of culture.

Polarizations in perceptions of culture

The common experience for therapists with refugees is to have all-or-nothing experiences in relation to culture. Either everything is put down to culture – 'They do this because it is their culture. They don't do that because it is their culture. They believe this, or don't believe that, because it is their culture' – in which case culture, or cultural difference, can appear to be a huge and unbridgeable gap; or culture is entirely absent as an issue and therapy proceeds as if there is a completely shared universal understanding in which cultural difference plays no part at all.

The debate about the fact that psychotherapy and counselling are themselves products of particular western, middle-class, intellectual cultures in Europe and the US often facilitates and encourages this sort of polarization. On the one hand the therapist finds him or herself accused of imposing an alien ideology or cultural form on dependent and vulnerable members of other cultures. On the other hand there are those who insist on the universality of the scientific insights of counselling and psychotherapy, claiming their applicability and appropriateness to all cultures and dismissing clients who do not accept their premises as not sufficiently psychologically minded to be suitable cases for treatment. The therapist, faced with this choice, is invited to choose between giving up, trying to offer therapy to people from other cultures, or denying that the cultural difference is something that needs to be taken account of and respected but perhaps not worshipped.

Many therapists will be people who have taken a critical stance in relation to their *own* culture and may well have waged various struggles within it. The idea of viewing a culture critically should not therefore be alien to them. However, many therapists find themselves being 'respectful' of other cultures to the point of reverence and idealization. While this avoids the tendency towards cultural imperialism, and allows clients to hang on to their cultural roots for as long as they need, it may prevent the therapist from thinking more critically and helping clients to free themselves from some of the constraints that the culture might impose. For example, belief systems which are unsympathetic or even condemnatory towards women who have been raped tend to be unhelpful to female rape victims and to their families. Obviously a direct attack on a client's culture is unhelpful, and clearly a lack of respect for cultural difference and cultural integrity can lead to forms of cultural imperialism. But it is possible to discuss the similarities and differences between cultures and the ways in which cultures change and revise their beliefs and values. And it is quite possible to respect another culture and a client's loyalty to it without feeling that it must be unquestioningly accepted as entirely virtuous or unchangeable.

The otherness of the 'other'

One of the great myths of modern counselling and psycho-therapy is the overestimation of the extent to which we can ever really understand another person. In much counselling and psychotherapy the experiences of therapists and clients have enough in common to support the myth. Encounters with members of a culture which is significantly different from our own make us more aware, and perhaps uncomfortably aware, of how difficult the task of understanding another, or even understanding ourselves, actually is.

CHAPTER 10

Interpersonal Level

The impact of clients' traumatic experiences

Most counsellors and psychotherapists coming into this field of work are surprised and often somewhat disconcerted by the intensity of the interpersonal encounter. Some of them, warned of this in advance, cannot believe that they are not already well prepared. They may have worked in acute psychiatric in-patient units, or have spent many years wrestling with intense transference and countertransference feelings in psychoanalytic work. Or they may have worked with survivors of disasters, victims of crime, domestic violence or sexual abuse, or with people suddenly and tragically bereaved.

All these experiences may be valuable and provide sources of understanding, insight, resilience and confidence on which the therapist can draw. But they are unlikely to have prepared him or her for the acutely traumatized survivors he or she may encounter among the refugee population.

Those who have witnessed and suffered some of the worst that human beings are capable of carry a strange first-hand knowledge of the human condition: things of which most of us have only a secondary knowledge. In many cases it seems that it might be this terrible knowledge, as much as anything else, that they want to escape, while at another level it is precisely that knowledge that they have to share with the therapists.

Therapists are therefore likely to experience powerful feelings in relation to the client. Particularly they are likely to experience a powerful pull to identification and conversely a powerful push to disidentification. They may feel many things on the clients' behalf, most commonly anger and outrage at the injustice the clients suffer, both in their own countries and the new country in which they seek refuge, but also great sadness and grief. They may also feel threatened by the power and intensity of the clients' feelings of rage, grief and despair.

One colleague described the look some of her clients gave her which made her feel she was the only person left in the world who could help them. It was a look she had not previously encountered in many years of working as a psychiatric social worker. This look is not unlike that of the totally dependent infant. It can induce powerful feelings of responsibility and protectiveness or, conversely, a wish to disengage in order to escape the weight of so much need.

However, there is another look which seems like that of someone returned from the dead: the haunted look of eyes that have seen unspeakable horrors, perhaps horrors that the mind can no longer remember. The client may at some level try to protect the counsellor from these memories and feelings. The counsellor can thus be feeling protective *of* the client while at the same time being protected *by* the client and perhaps feeling the need to be thus protected. Such an interaction if unrecognized can easily become locked into a static scenario of protective parent and compliant child/infant.

The depth of clients' suffering and their anger can also be experienced as intimidating. Clients can indeed be extremely angry with their therapists, turning on them the rage which they are powerless to express against those who have persecuted and tortured them in their homelands and those who doubt the truth of their accounts and deny them the basics of life and self-respect in their current situation.

However, there is also a less clearly articulated reproach against those who have not endured such suffering – those who have been privileged to live more comfortable lives and have been spared direct encounters with the worse elements of human savagery. Therapists can become acutely aware of this subtle sense of reproach (they may even imagine it when it is not there). And it is something which can be very difficult to talk about, not least because clients will usually deny it. Indeed it is often very difficult to address any sort of anger or criticism clients feel towards their therapists, largely because the clients feel so overwhelmingly grateful, appreciative, dependent and vulnerable. Therapists usually take a long time to feel comfortable exploring the actual details of violence and torture the client may have suffered. The result is a tendency to behave, as one colleague once put it, like swimmers entering a cold sea: they hold off for ages braving themselves, then run and dive in, in a great rush, trying to get through the shock and discomfort quickly. Having addressed the more painful and gruesome details of the client's experience in this way, there is then a tendency to feel that 'that bit has been dealt with' and to withdraw to less highly charged areas of the client's life such as the current difficulties of finding work, or the place where so many psychodynamic counsellors and psychotherapists feel most at home, the client's early life and family relationships. Once back on safe ground or 'dry land', the therapist may then feel that it is unnecessarily intrusive or cruel to attempt to make any connections between current problems or childhood relationships and the traumatic experiences of torture and violence. Thus client and therapist can come to collude in avoiding some of the things that most need to be talked about.

The impact of the refugee situation

Even where the refugees have not had direct encounters with shocking levels of violence, they have nevertheless come to fear for their lives in some way or other: so much so that they have taken flight and come into exile, which is often in itself a traumatic experience.

They are also likely to have left friends and family behind whom they will both miss and be worried about. Thus therapists can find themselves drawn into some of the same scenarios described earlier in relation to the more horrific events experienced by the clients and in relation to the other acute interpersonal losses and anxieties. Moreover, the therapist can readily become the interpersonal substitute for all the lost significant others in the client's life.

A colleague has described staff in a refugee agency as becoming terrorized by the poverty and deprivation suffered by their refugee clients in British society. The voucher system, homelessness and hunger, combined with the ever-present threat of deportation, have produced large numbers of clients whose basic needs the workers are quite unable to meet. Counsellors have not signed up to deal with this level of physical and material deprivation and are unused to it in their clients. It can readily lead to powerful feelings of helplessness and a sense of the uselessness of counselling or psychotherapy in such circumstances.

Another colleague once described to me his impulse to reach for his cheque book when his penniless client talked of the £500 that was needed to bring his family from Africa to join him in the UK. Seeing that so much of the client's pain, anxiety and distress might be alleviated if he could have his wife and child with him, and recognizing that all that was lacking was a sum of money that was relatively small in relation to the scale of suffering caused by its lack, my colleague experienced a powerful temptation. Indeed, it seemed he felt a powerful sense that it was in some way quite sadistic to sit and talk with the client about the pain caused by a practical problem in relation to which the client was quite powerless, but which the therapist could quite easily resolve.

Therapists may also feel a powerful sense of guilt and discomfort with regard to their government's overall treatment of refugees. Whatever the political and cultural realities may be, and however opposed the therapist may be to the government and the climate of opinion in which its policies are developed, it is still difficult in the immediacy of the interpersonal encounter for him or her not to feel in some way responsible for and representative of his or her society and its government. Others may feel confused and overwhelmed by the complexity of the refugee situation at a global level and the seemingly endless succession of wars and regressive government programmes which seem to go on producing refugees – a situation in relation to which their own government and the developed world in general seems to have little in the way of any coherent policy.

Conflict with colleagues

This is an area where political, cultural and intrapsychic levels can converge to overdetermine interpersonal relationships between colleagues.

The intrapsychic impact of the clients' experiences on the individual therapists can readily lead to those therapists becoming impatient and unduly combative with each other. This conflict may occur between colleagues within the same agency and with those in other agencies. It may also be fuelled by the culture and internal politics of the agency, which may in turn reflect the external political, social and economic pressures on the agency and on the refugee population.

The term 'personality clash' is often a reductionist explanation for interpersonal conflicts that are far more complex and multilayered. Colleagues do not have to like each other personally in order to work together and cooperate in a professional way. So most alleged personality clashes may be better understood in terms of:

1.   the impact of the work on the individuals involved

2.   what they might be expressing for subgroups within the agency, and perhaps for the agency as a whole

3.   the agency culture within which the conflict takes place

4.   the external social and political conflicts involving refugees both in their home countries and in the host country.

CHAPTER 11

Intrapsychic Level

Unconscious motivations and defences

Very few counsellors or psychotherapists who come to work at the Medical Foundation have very much idea of what, at a deep intrapsychic level, motivates them to engage in work with survivors of torture and organized violence. This suggests that such motivation exists in areas of the psyche barely touched on in training analysis or in previous psychotherapy or counselling.

It further suggests that undertaking this sort of work is a way of engaging with some of these outstanding issues. Most significantly it also suggests that the defensive structure surrounding these unrevealed areas of intrapsychic life may be particularly strong, deeply unconscious and hedged around with powerful resistance. This in turn may lead to a whole range of strange thinking, feeling and behaving in relation to the work which can be quite inaccessible to reflection and self-analysis.

Many therapists who find themselves working with refugees will not have chosen that particular client group but will have been chosen by it, or by the general circumstances of their work. They will not necessarily have the same sort of motivation as those who chose this field of work. Nevertheless the basic psychodynamics that become mobilized in this work are common to all of us; and they tend to be those dynamics that are particularly primitive, conflictual and difficult to access.

I assume that all psychotherapists and counsellors have their own defensive structures which they deploy in their work, of which they are more or less aware. Some of these are shared 'professional' defences; others are more personal and idiosyncratic. However, just as the violence and persecution the refugees have suffered can overwhelm their defensive structures, so too, in the therapeutic setting, it can overwhelm the habitual defences of the therapist, forcing him or her back into more primitive defensive strategies with which he or she may be less familiar and find it harder to recognize.

Therapists can thus believe they are coping well with what a client is feeling, while acting out their countertransference in completely unconscious ways. These may include:

- not keeping time in beginning or ending sessions and, instead of recognizing the significance of such breaches of the boundaries, explaining them away in any of a variety of ways

- cancelling appointments at short notice and failing to contemplate the impact this might have on clients

- breaches of confidentiality which they would not for a moment contemplate with their private clients, but which are justified in relation to refugees by claims about the need to act on the client's behalf, liaise with other agencies etc.

- home visits and social contacts similarly undertaken on the basis of quite tenuous reasoning or rationalization without any serious analytic reflection on what might be going on unconsciously between client and therapist or what specifically might be being acted out in the therapist's own unconscious.

The social unconscious

Then there is what group analysts call the 'social unconscious'. Most counsellors and psychotherapists tend to assume they are people with good liberal values and that they are opposed to racism and other form of discrimination. They tend to assume that such prejudices are the product of intrapsychic defence mechanisms and, having had a training analysis or something similar, they assume that they themselves do not routinely deploy such defences.

This is a dangerous assumption and quite mistaken. When we grow up in a culture we unconsciously internalize the beliefs and values of that culture. If, as is usually the case, some of those beliefs and values refer to people of other cultures, often prejudicially, then we take that in too. Any English person growing up in the UK in the twentieth century who believes there is no trace of 'empire' in the depths of his or her psyche, is in my opinion misleading him or herself. We live now in the age of the American Empire. Though it is an unofficial empire, it is the only one in history to be bigger than the British Empire, and its values and assumptions are everywhere: not only in the outside world of McDonald's, but in the ideologies of our businesses and professions, in the constitutions of the UK Council for Psychotherapists (UKCP) and British Association for Counselling and Psychotherapy (BACP) and in the psyches of most if not all counsellors and psychotherapists.

This sort of thing is rarely if ever discussed and analysed in training analyses – not least because analyst and analysand frequently share the same or very similar cultural backgrounds and assumptions, but also because psychoanalytic and psychodynamic thought has traditionally tended to ignore culture (except in specific psychoanalytic excursions into the field of anthropology), or at least to treat it as an epiphenomenon which can be reduced to psychodynamic explanations. These attitudes and conflicts are therefore likely to reside in areas of the psyche that have been scarcely touched in training analyses or therapy.

Being prepared to be unprepared

Similarly, other more common intrapsychic themes of abandonment, overwhelming pain and terror of psychic disintegration, while they may have been touched on in training analysis and therapy, may not have been explored in any great depth. Often, an ordinary analysis or psychotherapy may touch on these areas sufficiently to stir them up and create greater volatility without adequately understanding and appreciating their depth and intensity, and the defences mobilized in relation to them. It is one thing to recognize or even to struggle with fantasies or phantasies* of violence, destruction, abandonment or castration. But to come close to the translation of these phantasies/fantasies into reality is something quite different. How many analysands have wanted to kill their analyst? How many have actually tried to do it?

It is important to remember that many of the experiences of refugees are truly horrific. They are not the phantasied

---

*   For readers unfamiliar with this distinction: 'fantasy' is conscious, 'phantasy' is unconscious.

attacks of the infants on the mother, nor of the client on the therapist. Neither are they the interpersonal cruelties of domestic violence nor of the individual criminal. What refugees have encountered exists on an entirely different scale. The intensity of individual acts of violence can be highlighted by the relative tranquillity of the social context. But in the wars, genocides and state terror campaigns from which refugees take flight, the intensity of individual violence is vastly multiplied to an overwhelming level: a level which is implicit in the experiences of refugee clients. These experiences are not manageable or containable in any ordinary (whatever that means) way. They require substantial defences in both clients and therapists.

Therapists who believe they do not need such defences, or that they do not have any, are rather dangerous to themselves, and to the clients. Defences are necessary. What is important is to know that defences are necessary, to have some idea what they might be, and a readiness to reflect on a whole range of possibilities.

Part IV

Essential Additions:
Completing the Picture

CHAPTER 12

Working with Interpreters

Much counselling and psychotherapy with refugees involves working with interpreters. Therapists who have never worked with interpreters often find it hard to imagine how this can work. They become worried about not hearing first-hand what the client actually says and concerned as to whether they will be able to detect unconscious themes in the way they usually do. They also worry about having another person in the room and how this will affect the transference.

Critical superego or creative resource

When therapists first begin working with interpreters they tend to project their own critical superego onto the interpreter. Here is someone from the same country and perhaps the same refugee community as the client. He or she will naturally understand the politics, culture and probably the personal experiences of the client better than the therapist can hope to do. Moreover, the interpreter may have interpreted in hundreds of counselling sessions with refugees and have seen many different counsellors and psychotherapists at work. He or she therefore has a great deal of experience and knowledge against which to assess the therapist's performance.

Family therapists who have got used to having their supervisors and colleagues observing them 'live' in their therapeutic work may be less daunted by the situation. Group therapists too who are used to having their understanding and contributions assessed by half a dozen or more group members also have some useful experiences to draw on. But therapists who have only worked individually and have experienced only supervision by report and reflection can feel daunted. And even family therapists and group therapists have to deal with the fact that the interpreter is not the familiar figure of the live supervisor, nor is he or she in the somewhat dependent position of being another patient (as in group therapy), neither is he or she someone who shares the same theoretical model and approach to the counselling or psychotherapy. So the interpreter remains a potentially threatening figure at least until a working relationship has become established.

The answer to many of these difficulties is of course to draw upon the interpreters' knowledge and experience as a resource. Don't be intimidated by it. Use it. But do not use it uncritically or unquestioningly. Having admitted that the interpreter is a source of expertise it is easy for the therapist to allow the interpreter to take over and in some sense 'lead' the therapeutic process. It is therefore important to remember that the interpreter is not a counsellor or a psychotherapist – and if the interpreter is going to function as a sort of co-therapist, he or she needs to be a junior co-therapist. Interpreters will have their own concerns and anxieties and it is important that the therapist maintains the role of the person in charge of the therapy.

It is important for the therapist to spend a little time before working with a new interpreter to explain how he or she wants the interpreter to work. Does the therapist want exact interpretations of everything the client says? Does the therapist want to be warned if he or she is about to make a transcultural faux pas? Does the therapist welcome observations or opinion from the interpreter during the session or should these be kept to the end? Different therapists will have different preferences, and the interpreter needs to be given some clear guidelines by the therapist before they start work together.

It is also important to spend ten minutes with the interpreter after the session to discuss what has happened, to help the interpreter understand the work, to give him or her the opportunity to contribute ideas and insights, and to allow him or her to express the feelings which are likely to be evoked in the session. (If it is possible to spend longer than ten minutes, so much the better, especially if the interpreter is unfamiliar with this work.)

Therapists will be surprised how quickly they become comfortable working with interpreters. It is an axiom in the world of football that a good referee is distinguished by the fact that players and spectators forget he is there. The same is often true of interpreters in counselling and psychotherapy. A good interpreter is the one you become unaware of in the course of the session.

Language and communication

The language difficulty – that the client is speaking a different language from which certain nuances and double meanings must inevitably be lost in translation – is a relatively minor problem. Communication theorists have long recognized that the tone of voice and other elements of non-verbal communication – looks, posture, gesture etc. – are generally far more significant in the establishment of relationships and in communicating feeling than the actual words used, and these channels of communication are all readily available. They are, moreover, the channels through which projective identification is mainly achieved, and through which countertransference generally is evoked. Indeed the increased reliance on this level of communication at the expense of close attention to the actual words and sentence structure may well improve rather than detract from the levels of interpersonal and intrapsychic understanding.

Split transference?

Split transference is also much more of a problem in theory than in reality. As I have suggested in the sections on the interpersonal level, the refugee client is usually more in need of a witness than a transference figure. Transference is generally not something to be facilitated but something to be neutralized through reminding the client of the reality, and if necessary interpreting the way the therapist is being misperceived as a symbolic parent. Obviously there will always be transference as there is in any relationship and it cannot all be addressed but it needs to be kept at a manageable level as in an adult-to-adult relationship, not promoted in order to encourage regression as in the classical psychoanalytic model.

Authority and leadership

The interpreter may be very knowledgeable about the client's culture and political context, and may also understand the refugee community much better than the therapist. In some cases this can lead to the interpreter becoming the 'senior partner' and at times taking over the therapy. It is important that, while respecting the interpreter's knowledge and expertise, the therapist should be in charge of the therapy. If the therapist and interpreter are a two-person team, then the therapist must be the team leader and must be prepared when necessary to direct the interpreter.

White therapists working with non-white interpreters are sometimes inhibited in exercising this authority because of its uncomfortable echoes of empire. Others, less aware of such echoes, may direct the interpreter in a superior or condescending manner that *is* actually an echo of empire. Some therapists just have a problem with any sort of authority!

These dynamics can also be replayed in the agency itself where interpreters may be afforded too much power and influence out of an anxiety not to offend them, or they may be treated with a lack of respect and not afforded the equal status appropriate to professional colleagues.

Support and projection

In some agencies I have known, special support facilities have been provided for interpreters, because it was said that they were likely to be upset by the work because they came from the same persecutory political situation as the clients and the clients' experiences would resonate with their own. There was of course a good deal of truth in this assertion and it was a wise move to provide support for the interpreters. But the act of providing support *only* for the interpreters enabled the English professionals to deny the extent to which they were upset and disturbed by the clients' experiences, and to project their own difficulties and needs for support into the interpreters. Thus the effort to give special support to the interpreters paradoxically gave them an additional burden.

However, on the positive side, the issues raised by the presence of interpreters and the struggles involved in resolving or at least coming to terms with them provides learning and understanding which further informs the work with clients.

CHAPTER 13

Advocacy – Protection, Asylum and Welfare Rights

Asylum and protection

Counselling and psychotherapy are not going to help a refugee client very much if the client is sent back to his or her country of origin to be tortured or killed. So the therapist's first duty is to contribute whatever he or she can to ensure that the refugee has the best chance of staying in the host country and therefore staying alive. There is therefore a duty of protection as well as a task of listening and understanding.

The therapist needs therefore to check the progress of clients' asylum applications and check that clients have effective legal representation. The therapist may also be asked by a client's lawyer to provide a psychological assessment and report of the therapeutic work to support the asylum application. The therapist might even go so far as to make sure the lawyer involved knows that such a report can be made available, as it may not have been considered by a lawyer unfamiliar with asylum applications.

Obviously the client's anxieties about this whole process are likely to be prominent in the counselling or psychotherapy work. Therapists need to recognize that they are not dealing only with 'anxieties', but with anxieties based on a *real threat*. They need to note carefully whether the clients' anxieties, or defences against them, interfere with or prevent them from taking the most effective action in pursuit of their asylum application – for example, failure to monitor their lawyer's work, reluctance to change lawyer if dissatisfied with their service, failure to include important details of their persecution in their asylum application statement etc. Refugee clients can be too ready to put themselves in the hands of others and trust that they will be taken care of. This may sometimes be the other side of the coin from feelings of acute anxiety, mistrust, hypervigilance and even paranoia resulting from their experiences of betrayal and persecution.

General welfare rights and advocacy

In addition to obtaining asylum, refugees have to deal with other institutions of this society with which they are necessarily going to be unfamiliar. They have to claim their rights to income support, housing and education and most of them have to do this without being able to speak English. Moreover their experiences of becoming refugees may have affected their confidence and competence in dealing with institutions and officials, and of course their initial ability to deal with such issues will vary widely. Some who have been political activists, 'professionals' or administrators in their country of origin may have been highly skilled in this area, while others who have come from communities where there is little paperwork or bureaucracy may have little or no relevant experience on which to draw.

Given that the therapist may be the only member of the host community whom the refugee client feels he or she can really communicate with and trust, it is from that therapist that the client will seek advice and practical assistance in dealing with all the issues he or she feels unable to cope with. So, problems and misunderstandings with the National Asylum Support Service (NASS), local housing departments, schools, hospitals etc. are all likely to be brought to the psychotherapy/counselling sessions and the therapist may need to offer the relevant advice and even write the odd letter or make the odd phone call or two.

There is no clear guideline as to how much of this sort of thing a therapist should do because each individual case is different. The therapist must assess in each instance how far it is really necessary to intervene. Clients may be genuinely at a loss and have no-one else to turn to, or they may be lapsing into an unnecessary dependence on the therapist and be in need of encouragement to act on their own behalf, or perhaps in need of the sort of therapeutic intervention that addresses their feelings of helplessness and enables them to get in touch with their own capacities and abilities from which they may have become dissociated.

Again the question arises as to the nature and function of the therapist's agency. Are there other workers within the agency who can take on advocacy, protection and welfare rights work? Are there other organizations that can take it on and with which the therapist can liaise?

A trap to avoid

There is a not uncommon myth that it is pointless to attempt counselling or psychotherapy with clients who are preoccupied with their struggle to obtain asylum and in immediate fear of deportation, or who are homeless and hungry. This assertion is often backed up with references to Maslow's 'pyramid of needs' in which psychological needs for self-fulfilment, self-realization etc. only become significant after more basic needs for material well-being have been met. It can be tempting to fall into this way of thinking, since doing therapy with people in real danger or in conditions of real material deprivation can be a harrowing experience for the therapist. Nevertheless even a passing acquaintance with the behaviour of people suffering in prisons and concentration camps reveals the extraordinary lengths to which they will go and the extraordinary ingenuity which they will apply to give and receive emotional support, establish intimacy and exercise their imagination and creativity. So it is often under the threat of deportation or in the course of struggling to obtain food, clothing and shelter that clients most need help in recognizing and managing their emotions in order to struggle more effectively for survival. Any good military commander can testify that the most vital factors for soldiers in highly dangerous and threatening situations are retaining good morale and the capacity to think clearly. These are surely factors which counsellors and psychotherapists can address with refugees who are in effect 'under fire'.

CHAPTER 14

Supervision

The need for supervision

This work is highly stressful. It is not a good idea to attempt to do it without some sort of supervision. This may be done by consulting regularly with one or more peers, or it may be done in a group or individually with a formally designated supervisor. (The relative merits of different formats are discussed below.) But it does need to be done.

It can be tempting for experienced therapists who have worked with other highly distressed and acutely traumatized clients to believe they no longer need to be supervised. They may think they have been practising long enough and have been supervised enough in the past for them now to be able to go it alone. Or they may at least feel that they know themselves and their work well enough to know when they need to consult a colleague or seek a supervisor. However, there are a number of problems with this way of thinking.

First, there are aspects to this particular field of work that are not found in other forms of counselling or psychotherapy. So it is likely if not certain to raise issues and make demands on the therapist with which he or she is unfamiliar, both at the technical and personal level.

A wide knowledge of political history and contemporary politics in many different parts of the world is called for, as is knowledge about different cultures. Therapists can learn about a particular country from their clients, but the more colleagues that are consulted and the more collective experience they have, the more knowledge and understanding can be brought to bear on particular political and cultural issues.

Few therapists are familiar with addressing political contexts in the course of therapy. And although the recognition of cultural issues has a developing place in the world of psychotherapy and counselling, much of this work is still relatively unsophisticated. So there is a need for dialogue and reflection with colleagues away from the therapeutic encounters with clients.

As I have already suggested, the part played by politics and culture in the constitution of the therapists' own personalities and identities seldom receives much if any attention in their training analyses. So this work is highly likely to touch on areas of themselves, particularly perhaps the social unconscious in which they participate, with which they are unfamiliar.

Given that work with refugees may focus on extreme acts of violence and destructiveness deliberately perpetrated in reality (rather than in fantasy where therapists in 'the west' are more used to encountering it) it may resonate at deep and frightening intrapsychic and interpersonal levels in a way the therapist has not previously experienced.

Moreover, it is often the case that therapists, like people generally, deal with horrific experiences by repressing and dissociating. They can thus be quite unconscious of the effect the work is having on them, and can go on enacting these defensive manoeuvres in their work with clients, in their relationships with colleagues and in their personal lives.

It is thus easy to arrive at a situation where therapists are unconscious of a substantial range of their own experience, at political, cultural, interpersonal and intrapsychic levels. And of course their work with their refugee clients can become significantly influenced by their need to preserve their defences and maintain their ignorance. It is only when space is provided for these issues to be recognized by others and brought to their attention that they can be properly addressed.

Some readers of the last paragraph may say: but surely this is true of all counselling and psychotherapy, and it is the reason for having supervision generally? So I want to emphasize that, in my experience, this work with refugees can engender a degree of unconsciousness and resistance in therapists that I do not find in other areas of counselling and psychotherapy.

It is further worth noting that this may be to some extent a characteristic of work with traumatized clients generally. Some years ago a colleague and I conducted a workshop on 'counter-transference' at a conference of the European Association for Traumatic Stress Research. We were interested to discover how many of the participants reported that this issue was not addressed in their workplaces, and in some cases it was at home where their changed behaviour and enactment of the effects of the work was noticed.

Also noteworthy is the fact already mentioned in the introduction that this chapter on supervision was not part of the original draft of this book. Despite that draft being read by several highly experienced and respected colleagues who proposed various amendments and additions, no-one suggested that I had left out an important chapter. It was only a year and a half later that I realized that something very important was missing.

The process of supervision

Supervision provides an opportunity to apply the four-level framework to clients and to therapists, to explore their experiences and reactions at each of the four levels, including their experiences of each other. It also provides an interpersonal context in which themes from all of these levels may emerge through being enacted, or acted out, in the supervisory relationship.

It is also an opportunity for thinking and learning generally about the work and practising the application of this particular framework, both of which may be new to the therapist. Indeed this is a relatively new field to all of us.

Working with refugees, as we have already discussed, can involve a powerful presentation of dependency by the client. This dependency may involve all four levels of relationship:

- the political dominance of the 'west' over the part of the world from which the refugee has come

- the shared fantasy of the superiority of western culture, particularly its science and technology

- the interpersonal reality of a relationship between an established and relatively influential professional and an asylum seeker with very little knowledge of the host society and no influence within it

- the intrapsychic regression and transference evoked by the traumatic experiences and the therapeutic context.

This, combined with the horrific nature of the client's experiences and the real material dangers and difficulties he or she may be currently facing (deportation, acute poverty), can generate a powerful sense of responsibility (over-responsibility) in the therapist. This can produce a level of anxiety and a sense of urgency in the therapist and in the supervision such that an emphasis develops on *what to do* – how to address the client's immediate emotional and/or material needs – rather than on how to *understand* and how to *learn*.

This urgency can also produce a focus on the client at the expense of examining the therapist's experience at all the different levels and facilitating his or her learning. It is only when the therapist is particularly and obviously disconcerted that the countertransference is addressed, and then only the specific part of it that is immediately problematic.

A further consequence of the 'urgency' can be that only the 'urgent' worrying or problematic situations are presented for supervision. This quickly becomes a habit with the underlying assumption that supervision is an arena for crisis management and problem solving rather than for professional and personal learning and development.

It is therefore important to be aware of these pressures and their impact on the supervision process, and to keep in mind the wider purposes of supervision. It is then necessary to address the dependency, the urgency and the associated anxieties so that they can be sufficiently contained to allow space for more generalized thinking and learning. It also needs to be remembered that the urgency of the client's predicament can mask the anxiety of the therapist about problematic aspects of him or herself stirred up by his or her encounter with the client.

The framework of supervision

Supervision can take place one to one with a supervisor, between two peers, in a group conducted by a supervisor, or in a group of peers. One-to-one supervision is perhaps the most common form of supervision in counselling and psychotherapy, but in this context it has certain specific advantages and drawbacks.

The advantages are as follows.

1.   It allows more time for presentation and discussion of an individual therapist's work, so a therapist may well be able to present a high proportion of his or her work for scrutiny and discussion.

2.   Some therapists may find it a safer place to explore some of their personal reactions to the work, particularly where these involve difficult areas of their personal lives.

3.   The greater intimacy of the situation may evoke feelings in the therapist which are connected with the intimacy of his or her relationship with the client (especially where the client is being seen individually).

The disadvantages are as follows.

1.   It only introduces one other person's perspective and understanding (with regard to both client and therapist).

2.   There is only one other person to help contain the powerful feelings evoked.

3.   Where there is a formal supervisor–supervisee relationship, the absence of a peer presence can facilitate a reproduction of the client's intense dependency; thus a hierarchy is set up with a dominant–subordinate relationship between therapist and client which is then mirrored and all too easily affirmed by a similar dominant–subordinate relationship between therapist and supervisor.

Group supervision also has advantages and disadvantages, which are more or less the converse of those of the one to one.

The advantages of a group are as follows.

1. It pools together more different perspectives, ideas and funds of relevant knowledge. Moreover, while two people may share a similar blind spot, it is less likely (though not impossible) that a whole group will do so.

2. A group can generally contain more anxiety and distress than one other individual. And while it may initially feel more exposing and less safe, the discovery of similar experiences and anxieties among several colleagues can be hugely reassuring to therapists who start to feel their experiences are reflecting some problem or inadequacy unique to themselves.

3. Therapists are actively engaged in supervising each other within a relatively egalitarian context, so the potential for reproducing the dominance–subordination or active–passive patterns of the therapist–client relationship are substantially reduced.

The disadvantages mainly concern the limited amount of time available to each supervisee to present his or her work and the consequent requirement for the supervisees to contain their anxiety and use the group as a place to learn generally about the work and then to be able to apply that learning independently.

Other considerations involve practical issues such as it usually being easier to arrange a meeting of two people than to arrange one for more than two, or the fact that group supervision may be cheaper in terms of paying for a supervisor's time, or using room space/time. (One meeting of four people for 90 minutes occupies one room for 90 minutes. Four meetings of two people for 50 minutes takes 200 minutes of room time.) There is of course a question of availability of rooms of a suitable size for groups.

Overall I believe groups to be preferable. They fit the whole context better. Refugees emerge in a political context and raise major questions about culture and cultural transition. Both politics and culture are multiperson contexts and the experience of collective endeavour, of working as a team, as part of a multiperson unit seems to address that collective social dimension far more effectively than a dyadic situation. I also believe there is a collective strength available from the group experience which cannot be found to the same extent in supervision with one other person.

The other factor to be considered is whether to engage in peer supervision or to have the hierarchy of a designated supervisor who becomes, ipso facto, an 'authority figure'. My experience suggests that while the peer model avoids certain obvious problems with hierarchy at all four levels, it does not remove them entirely, and it makes considerable demands on the discipline and personal authority of group members who must exercise considerable responsibility, autonomy and self-authorization if the group is to function effectively as a container. A peer dyad is less demanding, but unless both participants have substantial knowledge and experience of the field they may struggle to cope with this deficiency. So, given the particular stresses of this work and the powerful un-conscious response therapists often have to it, my preference is for a formally designated supervisor. Hierarchy can contain as well as oppress. Making it democratically responsive and accountable may be more productive than abolishing it.

CHAPTER 15

Summary

It is worth reiterating at this stage that the foregoing is not intended as a prescription for how to do therapy with refugees. My aim has been to set out a framework, based on our experiences at the Medical Foundation, within which individual therapists can develop their own individual styles. I have avoided 'models' because I do not believe human individuals and human problems readily fit into prescribed models. Moreover, the efforts made to fit them onto procrustean beds often limit and distort perception of their lived experience and are alienating within the context of the therapeutic relationship. Models and theories, of whatever persuasion (psychoanalytic, Rogerian, integrative, systemic, existential, Gestalt, cognitive etc.), should be regarded as *indicative* as distinct from prescriptive. They can function as compasses which indicate directions that might be taken, as lenses through which experiential phenomena can be perceived and conceptualized, and as sources of ideas, questions and explanations. But ultimately one is left only with the facts of the client's lived experience and his or her encounter with the therapist and a context of choice as to how these facts are to be perceived, thought about, organized and indeed constructed.

Nor should it be assumed that any one model operated by one practitioner is the same as that same model operated by another. Individual characteristics cannot be homogenized by shared theories or belief systems. Therapy (whether it is group, family or individual therapy) remains a dialectical process between people. Their encounters with each other and their outcome are necessarily a product of what they each bring to the situation – in terms of their personalities, beliefs, theories and histories – and of the context in which they meet.

Rigorously applied models may be more functional where clients are in a position to make choices between several different models and decide which one they want to work with. However, in contexts where there is less choice it is the responsibility of the therapist to adapt models, theories and his or her habitual way of working to the needs of the specific clients in their specific contexts.

This book provides a framework for making those adaptations and for perceiving and understanding the experiences clients and therapists have of themselves, their environment and each other.

The framework is divided into four levels, which apply to both client and therapist. Because the processes which create the phenomenon of refugees are first and foremost political processes, the political level is necessarily the meta-level and the starting point for developing a comprehensive understanding of the refugee's position. Next comes the cultural level, which embodies the system of meanings, beliefs, values, language and communication within which both refugee and therapist will have separately evolved and continue to evolve as individuals with a personal identity and sense of 'self'. The unconscious aspects of these two levels can be regarded as constituting what group analysts call the 'social unconscious'. Within these large social contexts is the third level of interpersonal relationships through which cultural and political dimensions are mediated and within which individual personality is formed. Lastly we have the intrapsychic level where the physiological demands of the living organism meet the demands of social relationships and communal living, creating the specific conflict on which psychoanalysis was originally founded. This level is particularly important for people who have suffered torture, other forms of violence, or the death of family members or close friends, all of which trigger physiological responses with which the mind must then struggle. The use of the term intrapsychic should not be taken to infer that political, cultural and interpersonal factors are solely external. They are in fact internalized, often quite unconsciously, and form different levels in the individual mind as well as different levels in the collective social matrix. The levels also generate their own internal conflicts. And it is important to recognize that all these levels are recursively connected. Thus a single event may resonate at all four levels, and changes at one level may cause changes at other levels.

The last part of the book deals with two additional aspects of the context in which therapist and refugee encounter each other. The first is the immediate presence and involvement in the therapeutic process of interpreters. The second is the omnipresent context of the government policy and legislation with regard to 'asylum'. This affects refugees' material conditions in terms of accommodation, food, clothing, lack of opportunity to work, and crucially their sense of safety (or lack of it) as long as they remain uncertain as to whether they will be returned to the place of danger and possible death from which they have fled. The media-driven and government-supported climate of disbelief with its anxieties about 'bogus asylum seekers' and its preoccupation with reducing the number of refugees seeking asylum in the UK create a persecutory environment for the refugee which resonates with the persecution already suffered, and reverberates at all four levels of experience both for the refugee and for the therapist. Moreover it often requires the therapist to take some responsibility to ensure that the client's legal and material needs are being appropriately addressed if not properly remedied. It is difficult to pursue a course of rehabilitative therapy with a client who is hungry, homeless or deported. Once again the emphasis is on the flexible application of therapeutic expertise and its adaptation to the specific situation.

I left until the end the topic of supervision because it is a crucial place where the framework can be applied and all the issues raised in the preceding chapters can be brought into focus. I regard it as an essential part of the work to enable the sort of reflecting and learning that this book is intended to promote.

Further Reading

The volume of literature relevant to work in this field is not only large but also diverse. So, for ease of reference, I have grouped sources of further reading under various headings. Inevitably the list is selective, but I have tried to cover a wide range and to limit the total volume to a manageable size.

First, the literature on trauma and political violence contains the main pioneers in this field which was profoundly shaped by work with survivors of the Nazi holocaust against the Jews and survivors of the first atomic bombs. It also includes Ben Shepherd's book tracing the history of war trauma and psychiatry back to World War I, and the Latin American workers who were most articulate about the political context of the work.

The second section on the wider political context provides an introduction to the political history and contemporary political background to the persecutions and human rights abuses occurring around the world, many of whose victims become our clients. It may be unfamiliar territory for some counsellors and psychotherapists but it is invaluable for locating both client and therapist in a wider political context. It includes both historical studies and the annual surveys undertaken by human rights organizations.

The third section covers issues of culture: both its shaping of individual personality and experience, and its impact on the relationship between client and therapist. There is a large literature on this topic so what I have included is a highly selective sample.

The fourth section is on 'trauma'. This covers some of the literature on trauma as a general phenomenon or category, and includes work with victims of a wide variety of different traumatic experiences. I think it is dangerously mistaken to treat 'traumas' as if they are a homogenous category which can be abstracted from their specific contexts – a point well developed in one of the listed works by Patrick Bracken. Nevertheless, as long as that problem is kept clearly in mind there is something to be learned from work with people suffering from different sorts of traumatic experience.

The fifth section includes therapeutic work with refugees generally and covers a range of refugee experiences.

The sixth section provides an introduction to the experiences of refugee children whose specific needs are often overlooked.

The seventh section is a reference point for working with interpreters.

The eighth section includes a number of attempts to bring psychological understanding to bear on history and politics, and to explain political violence and oppression in terms of their psychological roots.

The ninth section lists a number of papers. A great deal of the literature in this field is published in counselling, psychotherapy and medical journals or in chapters in books of assorted articles. They are too numerous to attempt a comprehensive list, which would in any case be indigestible. So a relatively small number have been included as a starting point. A complete list of publications by Medical Foundation staff is available on request from the Medical Foundation.

The last section is a list of relevant journals.

Trauma and political violence

Cienfuegos, A. J. and Monelli, C. (1983) 'The Testimony of Political Repression as a Therapeutic Instrument.' *American Journal of Orthopsychiatry 53*, 43–51.

Davidson, S. (1992) *Holding on to Humanity*. New York: New York University Press.

Kordon, D. R., Edelman, L. I., Lagos, D. M., Nicoletti, E., Bozzolo, R. C., Siaky, D., Hoste, M. L., Bonano, O. and Kersner, D. (1988) *The Psychological Effects of Political Repression*. Buenos Aries: Sudamericana Planeta.

Krystal, H. (ed) (1968) *Massive Psychic Trauma.* New York: International Universities Press.

Lifton, R. (1968) *Death in Life – Survivors of Hiroshima.* New York: Random House.

The above texts constitute the major pioneering work on trauma and political violence. They essentially map out the field although their work is often overlooked in more recent texts. See also:

Basoglu, M. (ed) (1992) *Torture and its Consequences: Current Treatment Approaches.* Cambridge: Cambridge University Press.

Garland, C. (ed) (1980) 'The Survivor Syndrome Workshop.' Special issue of *Group Analysis.* London: The Group Analytic Society.

Graessner, S., Gurris, N. and Pross, C. (2001) *At the Side of Torture Survivors: Treating a Terrible Assault on Human Dignity.* London and Baltimore: Johns Hopkins University Press.

Peel, M. (ed) (2004) *Rape as a Method of Torture.* London: The Medical Foundation for the Care of Victims of Torture.

Scarry, E. (1985) *The Body in Pain: The Making and Unmaking of the World.* New York: Oxford University Press.

Shepherd, B. (2000) *A War of Nerves: Soldiers and Psychiatrists 1914–1994.* London: Jonathan Cape.

A history of the psychiatric diagnosis and treatment of traumatized combatants.

Suedfeld, P. (ed) (1990) *Psychology and Torture.* New York, Washington, Philadelphia, London: Hemisphere Publishing Corporation.

Van der Veer, G. (1998) *Counselling and Therapy with Refugees and Victims of Trauma: Psychological Problems of Victims of War, Torture and Repression.* Chichester: John Wiley and Sons.

Political context and history

Chomsky, N. (1988) *The Culture of Terrorism.* London: Pluto Press.

Chomsky, N. (1991) *Deterring Democracy.* London and New York: Verso.

Chomsky, N. (1993) *Year 501: The Conquest Continues.* London: Verso.

Chomsky, N. (1997) *World Orders, Old and New.* London: Pluto Press.

Chomsky's sustained critique of the domination and frequently terrorization of the 'third world' by the 'west' and particularly by the USA is essential reading for a full appreciation of the part played by the apparently democratic societies of the west in creating refugees.

Hobsbawm, E. (1962) *The Age of Revolution 1789–1848.* London: Weidenfeld and Nicolson. Reprinted by Abacus, London 1994.

Hobsbawm, E. (1975) *The Age of Capital 1848–1875*. London: Weidenfeld and Nicolson. Reprinted by Abacus, London 1997.

Hobsbawm, E. (1987) *The Age of Empire 1875–1914*. London: Weidenfeld and Nicolson. Reprinted by Abacus, London 2001.

Hobsbawm, E. (1994) *The Age of Extremes 1914–1991*. London: Michael Joseph. Reprinted by Abacus, London 1995.

Hobsbawm's quartet shows how the industrialization and development of Europe is inextricably linked with the colonization of the 'third world'. The continuation of this relationship in the form of 'post-colonialism' provides the context for many of the 'third world' dictatorships and conflicts which produce so many refugees.

Fanon, F. (1965) *Studies in a Dying Colonialism*. New York: Monthly Review Press. Reprinted by Pelican Books, London 1970.

Fanon, F. (1965) *The Wretched of the Earth*. London: MacGibbon and Kee. Reprinted by Penguin, Harmonsdworth 1967.

Fanon, F. (1968) *Black Skin White Masks*. London: MacGibbon and Kee. Reprinted by Paladin, Boulder, CO 1970.

Fanon's work is the major study of the psychological impact of colonialism and the internalization of an oppressive political and cultural context.

Canovan, M. (1974) *The Political Thought of Hannah Arendt*. London: J. M. Dent and Sons.

An introduction to a series of studies of political violence and oppression which links the political with the individual.

Amnesty International Report

Published annually by Amnesty International, London. Provides more or less up to date summary of the human rights situation in each country in the world.

Human Rights

Annual Report of the UK Foreign and Commonwealth Office, London.

New Africa Yearbook

Published by IC Publications Ltd., London. Summarizes political history of each and every African country.

The World Guide

Published annually by New Internationalist Publications, Oxford. Summary of recent political history of every country.

Culture, and transcultural psychotherapy and counselling

Bracken, P. (2002) *Trauma: Culture, Meaning and Philosophy*. London: Whurr Publishers Ltd.

Dalal, F. (2002) *Race, Colour and the Process of Racialisation*. Hove and New York: Brunner-Routledge.

Fanon, F. (1965) *Studies in a Dying Colonialism*. New York: Monthly Review Press. Reprinted by Pelican Books, London 1970.

Fanon, F. (1965) *The Wretched of the Earth*. London: MacGibbon and Kee. Reprinted by Penguin, Harmondsworth 1967.

Fanon, F. (1968) *Black Skin White Masks*. London: MacGibbon and Kee. Reprinted by Paladin, Boulder, CO 1970.

Fernando, S. (2002) *Mental Health Race and Culture*. London: Palgrave.

Kareem, J. and Littlewood, R. (eds) (1992) *Intercultural Therapy. Themes, Interpretations and Practice*. Oxford: Blackwell.

Khanna, R. (2003) *Dark Continents: Psychoanalysis and Colonialism*. Durham and London: Duke University Press.

Said, E. (1993) *Culture and Imperialism*. London: Chatto and Windus. Reprinted by Vantage, New York 1994.

Trauma

Bracken, P. (2002) *Trauma: Culture, Meaning and Philosophy*. London: Whurr Publishers Ltd.

Garland, C. (ed) (1998) *Understanding Trauma: A Psychoanalytical Approach*. Tavistock Clinic Series. London: Gerald Duckworth & Co.

Herman, J. L. (1992) *Trauma and Recovery From Domestic Violence to Political Terror*. New York: Basic Books. Reprinted by Pandora, London 1994.

Saakvitre, K. W. and Pearlman, L. A. (1996) *Transforming the Pain: A Workbook on Vicarious Traumatisation*. New York and London: W. W. Norton & Co.

Wilson, J. P. and Raphael, B. (1993) *International Handbook of Traumatic Stress Syndromes*. New York: Plenum Press.

Refugees

Ager, A. (ed) (1999) *Refugees: Perspectives on the Experience of Forced Migration*. London: Continuum.

Dokter, D. (ed) (1998) *Arts Therapists, Refugees and Migrants: Reaching Across Borders*. London and Philadelphia: Jessica Kingsley Publishers.

Papadopoulos, R. K. (ed) (2002) *Therapeutic Care For Refugees: No Place Like Home.* Tavistock Clinic Series. London and New York: Karnac.

Van der Veer, G. (1998) *Counselling and Therapy with Refugees and Victims of Trauma: Psychological Problems of Victims of War, Torture and Repression.* Chichester: John Wiley and Sons.

Refugee children

Blackwell, D. and Melzak, S. (2000) *Far From the Battle But Still at War: Troubled Refugee Children in School.* London: Child Psychotherapy Trust Publication.

Richman, N. (1998) *In the Midst of the Whirlwind.* Stoke on Trent: Trentham Books.

Working with interpreters

Shackman, J. (1984) *The Right to be Understood: A Handbook on Working with, Employing and Training Community Interpreters.* Cambridge: National Extension College.

Tribe, R. and Raval, H. (eds) (2003) *Working with Interpreters in Mental Health.* London: Brunner-Routledge.

Psychological approaches to political violence

De Zuluetta, F. (1993) *From Pain to Violence: The Traumatic Roots of Destructiveness.* London: Whurr Publishers.

Lifton, R. (1986) *The Nazi Doctors: A Study in the Psychology of Evil.* London: Macmillan.

Staub, E. (1992) *The Roots of Evil.* Cambridge: Cambridge University Press.

Volkan, V. (1997) *Bloodlines: From Ethnic Pride to Ethnic Terrorism.* New York: Farrer, Straus and Giroux.

Volkan, V. (2004) *Blind Trust: Large Groups and Their Leaders in Times of Crisis and Terror.* Charlottesville, VA: Pitchstone Publishing.

Papers and chapters

Blackwell, D. (1997) 'Holding, Containing and Bearing Witness: The Problem of Helpfulness in Encounters with Torture Survivors.' *Journal of Social Work Practice 11,* 2, 81–90.

Bracken, P., Giller, J. and Summerfield, D. (1995) 'Psychological Responses to War and Atrocity: the Limitations of Current Concepts.' *Social Science and Medicine 40,* 8, 1073–1082.

Bracken, P. and Gorst-Unsworth, C. (1991) 'The Mental State of Detained Asylum Seekers.' *Psychiatric Bulletin 15,* 657–659.

Bustos, E. (1990) 'Dealing with the Unbearable: Reactions of Therapists and Therapeutic Institutions to Survivors of Torture.' In P. Suedfeld (ed) *Psychology and Torture*. New York: Hemisphere Publishing Corporation.

Comas-Diaz, L. and Padilla, A. M. (1990) 'Countertransference in Working with Victims of Political Repression.' *American Journal of Orthopsychiatry 60*, 1, 125–135.

Gorell-Barnes, G. and Papadopoulos, R. (eds) (2001) 'Refugees.' *Context: The Magazine for Family Therapy and Systemic Practice 54*.

Khan, S. (ed) (2003) 'Changing Contexts Changing Minds.' *Context: The Magazine for Family Therapy and Systemic Practice 67*.

Laub, D. and Auerhan, A. C. (1993) 'Knowing and Not Knowing Massive Psychic Trauma: Forms of Traumatic Memory.' *International Journal of Psycho-Analysis 74*, 287–302.

Melzak, S. (1999) 'Psychotherapeutic Work with Child and Adolescent Refugees from Political Violence.' In M. Lanyardo and A. Horne (eds) *Handbook of Child and Adolescent Psychotherapy: Psychoanalytic Approaches*. London: Routledge.

Sabbadini, A. (1996) 'From Wounded Victims to Scarred Survivors.' *British Journal of Psychotherapy 12*, 4, 513–520.

Schlapobersky, J. and Bamber, H. (1987) 'Rehabilitation Work with Victims of Torture.' In D. Miserez (ed) *Refugees – the Trauma of Exile*. London: Martinus Nijhoff Publishers.

Solomons, K. (1988) 'A Contribution to the Theory of Dynamic Mechanisms of Post Traumatic Stress Disorder in South African Detainees.' *Psychology in Society 11*, 18–30.

Somnier, F. E. and Genefke, I. K. (1986) 'Psychotherapy for Victims of Torture.' *British Journal of Psychiatry 149*, 323–329.

Turner, S. (1989) 'Working with Survivors.' *Psychiatric Bulletin 13*, 173–176.

Vinar, M. (1989) 'Pedro or the Demolition: A Psychoanalytic Look at Torture.' *British Journal of Psychotherapy 5*, 3, 353–363.

Werbart, A. and Lindbom-Jakobson, M. (1993) 'The "Living Dead" – Survivors of Torture and Psychosis.' *Psychoanalytic Psychotherapy 7*, 2, 163–180.

Woodcock, J. (2001) 'Trauma and Spirituality.' In T. Spiers (ed) *Trauma: A Practitioner's Guide to Counselling*. London: Brunner-Routledge.

A list of all the publications by Medical Foundation staff can be found on the Medical Foundation website: www.torturecare.org.uk.

Journals

Forced Migration Review
Published by the Refugee Studies Centre www.fmreview.org

In Exile: The Magazine on Refugee Rights
Published by The Refugee Council www. refugeecouncil.org.uk/
publications

Index on Censorship
Published by Writers and Scholars International Ltd
www.indexoncensorship.org

Journal of Refugee Studies
Published by Oxford University Press in association with Refugee Studies
Centre http://jrs.oupjournals.org

Medicine Conflict and Survival (formerly *Medicine and War*)
Published by Medical Action for Global Security (Medact)
www.medact.org/pub_mcs.php

*Mind and Human Interaction: Windows between History, Culture, Politics and
Psychoanalysis*
Published by the Centre for the Study of Mind and Human Interaction,
University of Virginia (USA) in conjunction with International Universities
Press. www.healthsystem.virginia.edu/internet/csmhi/journal.cfm

The New Internationalist
Published by New Internationalist Publications Ltd. Monthly publication
on economic and political development and human rights in the 'third
world' and the involvement of the 'west' www.newint.org

Refugees
United Nation High Commission on Refugees (UNHCR).
www.unhcr.ch/cgi-bin/texis/vtx/publ

Refugee Survey Quarterly
UNHCR Centre for Documentation and Research, Geneva. Published by
Oxford University Press http://rsq.oupjournals.org
*Torture – Quarterly Journal of Rehabilitation of Torture Victims and Prevention
of Torture* .
Published by the International Rehabilitation Council for Torture Victims
(IRCT)
www.irct.org/usr/irct/home.nsf
(not published since 2003 but may resume – back issues available).

Resources

The following is a list of the main sources of further information at a national and international level. The Medical Foundation for the Care of Victims of Torture, in London, provides a book called *Torture Survivors' Handbook* which lists a large number of local services in various parts of the UK; this is available on the Medical Foundation website (see below). Additionally, local refugee and community organizations, local law centres and Citizens Advice Bureaux can usually be discovered through local searches or through the national organizations' websites listed below. See especially Harpweb which is set up for this purpose.

Therapeutic work with victims of torture and organized violence

International Rehabilitation Council for Torture Victims
Borgergade 13
PO Box 9049
DK-1022 Copenhagen K
Denmark
Tel: +45 33 76 06 00   Fax: +45 33 76 05 00
www.irct.org

Medical Foundation for the Care of Victims of Torture
Isledon Road
London N7 7JW
Tel: +44 (0)20 7697 7777   Fax: +44 (0)20 7697 7799
www.torturecare.org.uk

Medical Foundation North West
The Angel Healthy Living Centre
Chapel Street
Salford M3 6FA
Tel: +44 (0)161 839 8090   Fax: +44 (0)161 839 7020

Study of and therapy for trauma
Aberdeen Traumatic Stress Clinic and the Centre for Trauma Research
Grampian Primary Care NHS Trust Headquarters
Benachie
Royal Cornhill Hospital
Aberdeen AB25 2ZH
Tel: +44 (0)1224 557892   Fax: +44 (0)1224 403602
Email: s.klein@abdn.ac.uk

Centre for Trauma Studies/Traumatic Stress Service
Nottinghamshire Healthcare NHS Trust
Westminster House
598 The Wells Road
Nottingham NG3 3AA
Tel: +44 (0)115 952 9436   Fax: +44 (0)115 952 9487

Clinical Treatment Centre Traumatic Stress Service
Maudsley Hospital
Denmark Hill
London SE5 8AZ
Tel: +44 (0)20 7919 2969   Fax: +44 (0)20 7919 3573

Traumatic Stress Clinic
Camden and Islington Community Health Services NHS Trust
73 Charlotte Street
London W1 1LB
Tel: +44 (0)20 7530 3666   Fax: +44 (0)20 7530 3677

UK Trauma Group
www.uktrauma.org.uk
Information and directory of services relating to trauma including links to
the European and International Societies for Traumatic Stress Studies.

Organizations providing and collecting information on and campaigning for human rights internationally

Amnesty International
99–119 Rosebery Avenue
London EC1R 4RE
Tel: + 44 (0)20 7814 6200   Fax: + 44 (0)20 7833 1510
www.amnesty.org.uk

Association for the Prevention of Torture
Route de Ferney 10
PO Box 2267
CH-1211 Geneva 2
Switzerland
Tel: +41 22 919 21 70   Fax: +41 22 919 21 80
www.apt.ch

Human Rights Watch
2nd Floor
2–12 Pentonville Road
London N1 9HF
Tel: +44 (0)20 7713 1955   Fax: + 44 (0)20 7713 1800
www.hrw.org

International Rehabilitation Council for Torture Victims
Borgergade 13
PO Box 9049
DK-1022 Copenhagen K
Denmark
Tel: +45 33 76 06 00   Fax: +45 33 76 05 00
www.irct.org

Medical Foundation for the Care of Victims of Torture
Isledon Road
London N7 7JW
Tel: +44 (0)20 7697 7777   Fax: +44 (0)20 7697 7799
www.torturecare.org.uk

Minority Rights Group International
379 Brixton Road
London SW9 7DE
Tel: +44 (0)20 7687 8700   Fax: +44 (0)20 7738 6265
www.minorityrights.org

New Internationalist Publications
55 Rectory Road
Oxford OX4 1BW
Tel: +44 (0)1865 728181   Fax: +44 (0)1865 793152
www.newint.org

World Organisation Against Torture
OMCT Europe
Rue de L'Enseiglement, 91, B-1000
Bruxelles
Belgium
Tel/Fax: +32 2 218 37 19
www.omct.org

Organizations dealing with general refugee issues

Asylum Aid
28 Commercial Street
London E1 6LS
Telephone advice line: +44 (0)20 7247 8741
www.asylumaid.org.uk

British Red Cross
9 Grosvenor Crescent
London SW1X 7EJ
Tel: +44 (0)20 7235 5454
www.redcross.org.uk

Harpweb
www.harpweb.org.uk
A website for those working with refugees which can locate the available resources in any area of the UK.

Medical Action for Global Security (Medact)
The Grayston Centre
28 Charles Square
London N1 6HT
Tel: +44 (0)20 7324 4739   Fax: +44 (0)20 7234 4734
www.medact.org
A network of health professionals working with refugees and asylum seekers.

Refugee Action
Head Office
The Old Fire Station
150 Waterloo Road
London SE1 8SB
Tel: +44 (0)20 7654 7700   Fax: +44 (0)20 7401 3699
www.refugee-action.org.uk

The Refugee Council
3 Bondway
London SW8 1SJ
Tel: +44 (0)20 7820 3000
www.refugeecouncil.org.uk

The Refugee Studies Centre
Queen Elizabeth House
21 St Giles
Oxford OX1 3LA
Tel: +44 (0)1865 270722
www.rsc.ox.ac.uk

The Scottish Refugee Council
5 Cadogan Square
170 Blythswood Court
Glasgow G2 7PH
Tel: +44 (0)141 248 9799   Fax: +44 (0)141 243 2499
www.scottishrefugeecouncil.org.uk

Spirasi
213 North Circular Road
Dublin 7
Tel: +44 (0)1838 9664   Fax: +44 (0)1868 6500
www.spirasi.ie

The Welsh Refugee Council
Phoenix House
389 Newport Road
Cardiff CF24 1TP
Tel: +44 (0)2920 489800

Tracing missing family

The British Red Cross, together with the International Committee of the Red Cross and Red Crescent Societies, can try to trace and establish contact with missing family members in the country of origin or in other countries they may have escaped to.

International Welfare Dept
British Red Cross
9 Grosvenor Crescent
London SW1X 7EJ
Tel: +44 (0)20 7235 5454
Email: iwd@redcross.org.uk
www.redcross.org.uk

Advice on accommodation, housing and welfare rights
Citizens Advice Bureaux
www.citizensadvice.org.uk
Locate local bureau from website.

National Homelessness Advice Service
Email: enquiries@nhas.org.uk
www.nhas.org.uk
Internet-based advice service.

Shelter
Tel: freephone 0808 800 4444 (24 hr)
Email: info@shelter.org.uk
www.shelternet.org.uk
Free advice on housing issues:
www.shelter.org.uk/advice/housingadvice.cfm
Internet-based advice service.

See also the refugee organizations listed above.

Legal advice
Law Centres
Local Law Centres can be found from www.lawcentres.org.uk

Liberty
21 Tabard Street
London SE1 4LA
Tel: +44 (0)20 7403 3888   Fax: +44 (0)20 74075354
www.liberty-human-rights.org.uk

Redress
87 Vauxhall Walk
London SE11 5HA
Tel: +44 (0)20 7793 1777   Fax: +44 (0)20 7793 1719
www.redress.org
Provides legal advice and assistance to individuals seeking reparation for torture.

Refugee Legal Centre
153–157 Commercial Road
London E1 2DA
Tel: +44 (0)20 7780 3200   Fax: +44 (0)20 7780 3201
www.refugee-legal-centre.org.uk

Therapists seeking advice on writing reports for lawyers to support asylum applications can also consult the Medical Foundation (see earlier for address).

Index

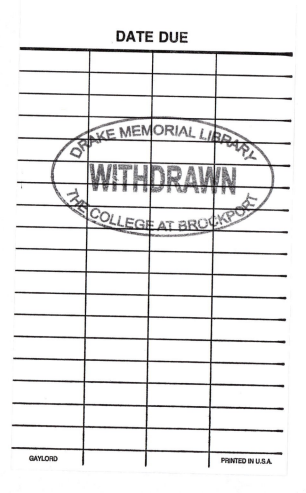